Positive Childhood

Mildred Masheder MA, Ac.Dip.Ed. is a former primary teacher and lecturer in child development and multicultural studies at what was the Polytechnic of North London. She subsequently held a research fellowship exploring cooperation and peaceful conflict resolution with children and is the author of a number of books, including *Let's Co-operate, Let's Enjoy Nature, Freedom from Bullying, Windows to Nature*, and the play section of *Natural Childhood*. She has also produced a video on cooperative play and parachute games.
She has two children and two grandchildren.

Positive Childhood
Educating Young Citizens

A Resource Book for Teachers and Parents of
Primary School Age Children

Mildred Masheder

GREEN PRINT

© Mildred Masheder, 2004
The author asserts the right to be identified as the
author of this work

First published 2004 by Green Print
an imprint of
The Merlin Press
PO Box 30705
London WC2E 8QD
www.merlinpress.co.uk

British Library Cataloguing in Publication Data
is available from the British Library

ISBN. 1854250949

Printed in Great Britain by Antony Rowe Ltd., Chippenham

Dedication

To Susanna, Mani, Sophie and George
With Love

From the Archbishop of Canterbury

No one can now ignore the urgency of the question of how we begin to introduce our children to the public world in a way that brings home the significance of clear values, strong commitments and generous attitudes. This book will be a welcome reminder of our responsibilities here, and a stimulus to thought and action.

Rowan Williams, Archbishop of Canterbury, Lambeth Palace, London.

Acknowledgments

My heartfelt thanks to Nicholas Gillett who gave me the inspiration to write this book.

To Guadalupe G. de Turner for her invaluable support in preparing and editing the manuscript and taking the photographs.

To the Gandhi Foundation, whose contribution on Peaceful Conflict Resolution was invaluable.

To the World Education Fellowship (WEF-GB) for their support and advice.

To Stifford Clays Junior School and Forty Hill C of E Primary School for their contribution and photographs.

To the Joseph Rowntree Charitable Trust and the Southall Trust for their continued support.

To the many parents and teachers who have helped me with good advice in the writing of this book, a special thank you.

To the Peace Movement, to which the book makes a small contribution.

Contents

Foreword

Brilliant! That was my reaction when I read this book. This engaging, practical guide enables the reader to enter into a personal reflective dialogue to consider how best to enable children to be happy, caring and positive citizens.

For a number of years Mildred Masheder has reminded us, in her insightful books, of the vital importance of childhood as a discrete stage of human development. For her, a society that fails, through its home life and schools, to nurture the early years of childhood, fuels a destructive fire of disaffection. As Mildred illustrates, the unhappy consequences of a lack of emotional literacy, coupled with a basic misunderstanding of universal values such as love, respect and care, can too often be seen in our society. Above all, her book is a celebration of childhood and the rich possibility for us all to act positively, not only to children but also to ourselves. The practical ideas in the book fill me with excitement because they reflect an approach to childhood that is natural and affirming. Readers are invited to feel empowered to take appropriate action, rather than castigated or blamed for current social ills. We are invited to consider a comprehensive range of techniques and possibilities that build into a comprehensive system of support for both parent and teacher.

Mildred's book builds on what we are beginning to understand about how our brains work. Especially how a lack of love and nurturing in the early stages of a child's life leads to a lack of growth in a part of the brain. This part of the brain is the 'gut reaction' part that controls responses. When the child is not nurtured and loved sufficiently this part of the brain does not mature – and therefore neither do the child's emotional responses. To grow into stable and confident adults, most children who have been labelled as having behavioural problems actually desperately need adults who will love, understand and care for them. If children feel loved and understood they become more confident and their self-esteem rises, and consequently they engage successfully in learning. In other words, we need to love the children in our care. Crucially, if we love and support children they too will learn to love and grow to be caring citizens. Teachers and parents are encouraged to work closely to develop supportive partnerships with children, considering ways in which they can be supported to understand with their feelings.

Flowing naturally from her understanding of the child's emotional world, Mildred firmly underpins the content of her book with a deep sense of the importance of enabling children to develop positive values in their lives. She appreciates that values are not taught but caught! However, in order for them to be caught, opportunities need to be created in both home and school for children to experience what a value means and how it can be applied in their lives. It has been found in school communities in Oxfordshire and elsewhere that in order to nurture values education a number of conditions need to exist. Firstly, teachers consider that it is vital that, in creating a values-based approach to teaching and learning, pupils are given help to develop appropriate behaviour. Aspects include:

- how to sit still and be comfortable in order to give your attention to the teacher;
- how to be relaxed yet alert in order to learn effectively;
- understanding that we all use body language to express ourselves;
- how to walk in the school in a quiet, purposeful and peaceful way;
- showing respect for self and others.

As a young infant needs to be toilet-trained, so do all children need to be supported in order to develop a positive attitude to learning. Boundaries of behaviour need to be set, otherwise the child is not free to develop self-discipline.

Parents and teachers who give positive reinforcement to children who display acceptable behaviour promote this basic training. This acts as a firm foundation for children to learn how to be responsible for their own behaviour. As Mildred indicates, paying attention to inappropriate behaviour has negative consequences. Adults need to concentrate on using positive language, thereby giving positive reinforcement. For instance, a teacher does not say: 'Why can't you at the back line up properly?' Instead she points out the child who is lining up correctly. Time invested in this basic attitudinal work is time well spent as it creates a school climate that is calm, purposeful and happy.

Developing good relationships between children and between adults and children is vital in creating the climate for them to take responsibility for both their learning and their lives in general. The adult's responsibility is to focus on developing an attitude of mind in children that encourages this. Pupils and adults need positive affirmation. The ideal atmosphere, both at home and in the classroom, supports the notion that adult and child are partners. This attitude creates a feeling of equal respect and a relationship of working together.

Mildred's book reminds us that the adult acts as the role model for the child. Children copy the attitudes and behaviour of adults – both good and bad. It is therefore important for parents and teachers to consider how they act as role models. For instance, the tone of our voice, the degree to which we are authentic in our interactions with children. In adopting a values-based approach there is no doubt that the ability of adults to model expected child behaviour is key to the development of positive behaviour. There is little point in talking about the value of respect if adults experience difficulty in respecting children!

It is also important to create quiet, reflective times at home and in the classroom. At school, a period of silence at the beginning of a lesson followed by a simple reflection, when the children are asked to consider and reflect on the work that they are about to do or have completed, is an excellent technique to develop positive thinking skills. While at home, times for stillness, quiet and reflection can be nurtured in the family, making it a regular 'activity'. The use of visualisation also develops the imaginative side of the brain that promotes creativity and problem solving. Periods of stillness help to create a learning-centred atmosphere that allows each child the opportunity to achieve success. The classroom's quiet and reflective atmosphere is not something that is imposed but grows out of the expectations and behaviour of the teacher. A more reflective atmosphere can be promoted, especially in more challenging classrooms, by using appropriate music during working periods that helps develop a peaceful atmosphere.

Mildred refers to the practice of Circle Time. There are various ways of promoting this valuable activity in the classroom. Such times give pupils the opportunity to articulate their thoughts and feelings and develop skills such as listening and empathy. It also gives the teacher an opportunity to enable the pupils to progress in their thinking, by asking questions that encourage the development of ideas. A technique that is useful is to create a forum theatre when a child requires advice. The way to do this is to ask the child to sit on a special chair while other children help the child to solve the problem. This encourages members of a peer group to help each other and, again, develops listening skills. The role of the teacher is crucial in this work as she or he helps the children to develop their thinking by asking questions. It is also important to use moments in the classroom to have conversations with individuals, or groups of pupils, to help them deal with issues that have arisen during the day. Staff should not feel guilty about taking time out of formal lessons to address matters of class concern. Obviously the judgement of the teacher is of paramount importance, ensuring that formal curriculum time is not wasted.

I believe such ideas, and all the excellent ones illustrated by Mildred Masheder in her gem of a book, are central keys that open the door to positive adult/child relationships which lead to a fulfilled childhood that acts as the foundation for positive citizenship and personal contentment.

Happy reading!

Neil Hawkes, Senior Education Adviser, Oxfordshire, UK.

Introduction

'Childhood! Winged likenesses half-guessed at, wheeling, oh, where? oh where?'
From *Childhood* by Rainer Maria Rilke, translated by J.B.Leishman.

Parents and teachers and anyone who is responsible for young children want to give them a happy and positive childhood. This is their birthright and the foundation for their future life. In modern living there are a number of factors that threaten the full realisation of the development of the whole child; the purpose of this book is to recapture a childhood which is based on their individual needs, and to lead them towards a fulfilled life in the family and as good citizens in the community.

We need to help children in their personal and social development from a very early age. How do they evolve from the ego-centric view of their world to one embracing other viewpoints with empathy and understanding? Certainly, they must be at peace within themselves to be able to reach out to other people. This is a long, slow process, but they are born with the ability and the urge to get on well with those around them and when this is beginning to work they will be able to think in terms of the wider community, which is the essence of good citizenship.

First and foremost they need to be able to deal with their emotions: nourishing the positive and acknowledging the negative ones. It is particularly important for children (and indeed adults) to be able to express their feelings openly, and it is only recently that the British as a whole have been aware of the need to say what they feel in a situation. The key is the realisation of a good self-concept, without which their whole well-being is seriously undermined. Their ability to talk about their feelings will be a major factor in their social development and in sharing their play they will be forging new relationships by means of dialogue.

Closely related to the open expression of the emotions is the gift of speech and the ability to communicate: talking of their feelings in Circle Time and at home; being able to state their case clearly and coherently in matters of opinion, in debate and in any dispute.

It is play and creativity that is the focal point of childhood and children come provided with an overwhelming desire to fashion their own world through play and in doing so make sense of their lives. Since they instinctively know how to create their own development, our role is one of support and encouragement, providing stimulation when needed and then letting them get on with it.

But modern life presents huge challenges to the natural heritage of childhood: our lives are continually changing and although there are benefits from modernisation, it is now not so easy for children to follow the natural patterns of development. The invasion of television and computer games into the home can erode the time for creative play and contact with nature, and even the most play-conscious parents experience dilemmas when confronted with their offsprings' insistent preferences for the electronic world. This way of life tends to curtail their social encounters, with a resulting impoverishment of their full language development.

Linked to the incursion of the electronic industry is the more general aspect of the penetration of commercialism into the lives of children. The whole philosophy of materialism is used to persuade them that happiness is gained through possessions, whether clothes, toys, the latest mechanical devices, etc. Young children are targeted to 'pester' their parents to buy, buy, buy for them and, influenced by the insidious publicity, they are led to believe that their aim should be to grow up as soon as possible so as to be able to have the privileges and possessions of adults. (In fact the adults are more likely to be trying to meet the latest credit card bill.)

Finally, there is the picture of life as extremely violent, as portrayed to children in everyday life, the news and, especially, television and computer games. Since they model themselves on the behaviour they see, it would be surprising if they emerged unscathed from these influences.

Furthermore, even at preschool level teachers are faced with pressure to concentrate on the so-called 'basics', although there has been some easing of the educational requirements at the youngest age level. This attitude of concentrating on the cognitive has been the bane of institutionalised education since it began, but at last it is beginning to be challenged forcefully by the concepts of 'multiple intelligences' and 'emotional literacy'. We now have these convincing theories and it is up to us as parents and teachers to challenge this short-sighted and mechanical approach to learning.

To be logical one has sometimes to state the negative which needs to be challenged and transformed in order to be positive and this is when we can counter these bad influences by introducing good value systems into education both at home and at school. Although we cannot dictate what values children finally adopt, we can teach them through activities, stories and discussion, and of course through our example and the moral values that we choose to provide as the basis for their behaviour and conduct.

For far too long there has been a negative approach to the teaching of behaviour; it has seemed easier for adults to point out what is wrong and unacceptable rather than to encourage and reinforce the positive. As this can happen both at home and at school it is likely that the recipients will not have a good opinion of themselves, since it is often not made clear that it is the action that is unacceptable and not the person. The very word discipline has an austere ring about it: one that inculcates fear rather than goodwill to do better. So our approach is above all to be positive: to praise when conduct deserves it, to indicate better ways of conduct through discussion on an equal basis and, most importantly, to aim at self-regulation and responsibility.

Before we tackle one of our main aims – that of teaching how to resolve conflicts peacefully – we need to concentrate on how children can come to terms with differences in others, whether racial, gender, age, culture patterns, class or disability. They need to be aware of the feelings of people who are discriminated against and to be able to protect themselves when they are the targets.

The emphasis on peaceful conflict resolution will include all the attributes already worked on: to deal with one's emotions, particularly anger, on the one hand, and feelings of inferiority on the other. The ability to state one's case clearly and to listen actively is vital in any attempt at mediation; and creative imagination is the basis of finding a solution which makes both parties satisfied. Experience in seeing the other's viewpoint does not come easily, especially for younger children, but this is a keynote in any kind of negotiation. As for positive behaviour and values education, it is no use trying to go through the motions of conflict solving if one hasn't the back-up of carefully drawn boundaries and a solid values policy. If all these factors come into play on an established basis and are consolidated by regular activities and games, serious conflicts should be reduced, with the whole of the community pledged to keep them at bay.

Finally, we can put our children on the right paths towards becoming responsible citizens and playing an active part in the affairs of the community. Once they have had their say and been listened to on a day-to-day basis, they will be more likely to make their opinions felt when they are adults and can participate fully in democratic procedures. If they have had the opportunity to make their own rules and to vote for their representatives on school councils, and if they are aware of the rights and responsibilities that accompany them, they will not easily let go of these privileges.

This journey towards maturity is never plain sailing, but the close cooperation of parents and teachers and other adults around them can enable children to grow up, with dignity and a true sense of self, to be responsible members of the community.

It is a journey that can be fun: children enjoying active learning and true participation with the help of the many ideas and suggestions in each chapter; these can be supplemented by the activities and games in my other books, which are listed in the bibliography. In playing together we can recapture the child within ourselves and share children's enthusiasm for life when they are able to develop naturally.

Chapter I

Expressing our Emotions

'… those first affections,
Are yet the fountain-light of all our day.'
*from **Ode on intimations of immortality from recollections of early childhood.***
William Wordsworth

This book begins with a heartfelt plea to give priority to the expression of the emotions. If we are sincere about bringing up children to become good citizens, we are committed to acknowledge the vital role played by their feelings. For far too long the process of learning has been solely concerned with the mistaken view that the mind is separate from feelings and only imbibes facts and information.

At last the enormous importance of the emotions in the development of children and young people is being recognised. Positive emotional well-being is the basis of their social development, and it is also the main influence on their ability to learn. Until recently the emphasis has been on the cognitive aspect of schooling; the role of the emotions has been greatly discounted. We may have progressed from the belief in the rigid application of the so-called intelligence quotient, but in most children's education there is little acknowledgement of the many other facets of their personality which are equally important.

Two pioneers have revealed this completely new concept of the whole child: Howard Gardner (1999) in formulating at least seven 'intelligences', and Daniel Goleman (1996) in his book *Emotional Intelligence: Why it can matter more than IQ*. Goleman has made a big impact with his emphasis on the power of the emotions, which should certainly equal and probably surpass the solely cognitive approach. He adds a further 'intelligence' to Gardener's seven – 'relationship intelligence' – and he continually stresses that emotional intelligence can have an enormous influence in improving standards, which is the present government's stated aim in the education system. He asserts that emotional literacy is in fact a core competence, guiding students into reasonable choices in areas such as personal relationships, learning and problem solving.

The qualities that Goleman includes in emotional intelligence are self-awareness, empathy, impulse control, self-motivation and self-discipline, compassion and altruism, and these are the aptitudes that make for good relationships. What is so important to parents and teachers is that these characteristics can be nurtured and strengthened throughout childhood, starting at birth and continuing well into adolescence. Moreover, a big plus for the human race is that we do seem to be born with a natural empathy towards others: Goleman cites extensive research showing how small babies seek comforted themselves when they see another baby upset, and then, at the age of one, when they realise that the unhappiness is not theirs, they tend to imitate the distress themselves and even try to get help by bringing their mother to give comfort to the other child. By about two and a half years old their empathy seems to depend on whether their parents have frequently drawn attention to how their misconduct causes distress to someone else: then they are more likely to show sympathy themselves, for example, they might offer a sweet or their favourite teddy bear. Similarly, if they are brought up in an atmosphere of seeing how others are willing to be of help to someone in distress, they are inclined to do the same. This is just one more example of how imitation of the adults around them plays such a significant part in their upbringing.

Although we may not have any inkling of the complicated function of the brain, recent research in this area does much to inform and help us in our dealings with children. We have always known that people learn best when they are experiencing

states of emotional well-being and we have also been aware that the two halves of the brain complement each other: the right side being primarily concerned with a holistic approach to intuition and creativity and the left side with language, numeracy and logic. In her book, *Developing the emotionally literate school* (2000), Katherine Weare reports on new research that is throwing light on whole brain approaches and the links that can be made with styles of learning. This research shows a clear connection between the emotions and learning. She reports that in recent years we have grasped the key role that the emotional side of the brain plays in any learning activity beyond simply absorbing facts, and that, by using our imagination, intuition and creative hunches, we are finding ways of connecting up the whole brain.

One aspect of this new research on the functioning of the brain is particularly relevant to the value of positive thinking: it appears that the limbic system, which controls the emotions, acts as a kind of switchboard, determining the information that goes to the 'thinking brain', the neo cortex, and that positive emotions facilitate such passage, whereas negative ones restrict it. Therefore, if we have lots of experiences in a supportive and encouraging context, we build up a rich network of connections in the brain and learning becomes easier. So we can be reassured that by creating a positive atmosphere and by openly exploring feelings we are developing a holistic approach to learning, with both the cognitive and the affective interacting. Although we might not be in a position to confirm these research results, they are common sense, for, as we all know, our emotions have a tremendous effect on our actions, our thinking and our general ability to acquire knowledge, and the proof of the power of positive thinking endorses our belief in its importance.

An organisation which has done much to promote the overwhelming influence of the emotions is 'Antidote: Campaign for

Emotional Literacy', which provides training and consultancy on how schools can use emotional literacy to promote achievement, positive behaviour and the well-being of staff as well as students. It is encouraging to hear that finally the DfES is encouraging schools to foster cultures which 'actively promote all children and staff's emotional well-being'. Antidote is conducting similar campaigns for parents and in the wider field of the workplace.

Translating the evidence of the important role of the emotions in the development of children into our endeavours to educate them, there is much that we can do. We can help them to deal with their feelings of anger and their fears and especially their relationships, so that they can grow up feeling good about themselves.

A good self-concept is the cornerstone of every child's development; it touches virtually all issues dealing with children and is the basis of their emotional and social well-being. Families and schools can provide us with close and intimate relationships that nurture feelings of belonging and security, support and sustenance; then children grow up with self-confidence, respect for others and an ability to express their emotions appropriately. If they do not they are more likely to become disaffected, violent or depressed.

So how do we, as parents and teachers, help our children to develop a strong sense of self-worth and a secure identity? We can certainly affirm them by acknowledging the good and admirable qualities that they possess. We can give encouragement and show interest in their endeavours and engage in purposeful conversation with them and listen attentively to their opinions. Ours is a competitive culture with many more losers than winners and it is all too often a 'put down' society; but we can always concentrate on positive rather than negative comments on their behaviour, using 'I' messages rather than the more accusative 'you'. This process of affirmation is important throughout the whole of childhood and the rebellious teenager needs it just as much as younger children. They can easily get the wrong messages if we seem to be everlastingly correcting them rather than responding positively and approving of their efforts. Right from the start they can easily feel, 'What's wrong with me?' and their whole sense of self-worth can be diminished.

Affirmation also means treating children with real respect, the sort you would give to a respected adult: the respect that would reach out to affirm their individuality and their unique personality, and, in their learning, respecting what and how they prefer to learn.

Every child is born capable of loving, celebrating and contributing to the world and the people in it, and, if this is nurtured and allowed to grow, they will accept themselves and feel accepted by others. Some children may be shy by temperament, but they can outgrow their timidity by support and understanding from the adults around them. What goes for children goes for us too; our ideal is to have such a secure self-concept ourselves that nothing can shake our conviction that we are 'good enough' parents and teachers, that we are doing our very best. That reassurance will certainly be sensed by and reflected in the children in our lives.

Expressing Feelings

Words expressing feelings: Brainstorm all the words that express feelings that you can think of. In small groups try to sort them out under headings: anger, fear, happiness, friendship, etc.

I feel happy when: In small groups make a tableau of each one's example of happiness: e.g. a birthday party, when I've painted a lovely picture, in bed listening to a story.

Do the same with other feelings: e.g. I feel peaceful when ...; I feel sad when .... Besides making tableaux, children can devise short

11

scenarios and act them out as mime or with improvised speech.

Guessing feelings: With the tableaux or mimes as described above, the spectators guess the emotions.

Feelings expressed through body language: What body language would show that you were – happy, sad, angry, afraid, etc.? Walk around in a spacious room and when the facilitator calls out a feeling act it out without touching anyone, then change as another emotion is called out. Discuss afterwards how you felt and whether the acting of the emotion had an effect on you.

Emotions in colour: What colour do you associate with the various emotions? Red for anger? blue for sadness? Paint abstracts or pictures of the various emotions. This is best done with large sheets of paper and powder paints for spontaneous expression.

Statues: In pairs, mime an emotion with your whole body; the partner guesses what it is. Next the partner can try to change the emotion by altering the stance and facial expression.

'I' and 'You' statements: Explain the difference between 'I' and 'You' statements: 'You' statements will probably cause the listener to feel accused or blamed, whereas 'I' statements express the needs and/or concerns of the speaker who can say 'I' feel (stating feelings) and then 'because …' (what happened). Practise in pairs an imaginary conflictual situation followed first by 'You' statements and then 'I' ones. A further exercise to show what a difference the emotional tone makes is to have a jokey 'You' message and a blaming tone 'I' message. Tone is all important in expressing feelings.

Dealing with fear: Make a list or tell a partner of all the things that make you afraid. What were you afraid of when you were small that is not frightening any more? (e.g. giants, monsters, wolves.) What can you do about things that still make you afraid? e.g. the dark (have a torch to switch on or a night light); thunder and lightning (count to see how far away it is); strangers – adults will tell the rules: e.g. not speaking or accepting anything from them; fear of speaking up in Circle Time; your opinion is just as valuable as everyone else's.

Underlying fears: Fear of separation from and death of loved ones are underlying in most children's minds and are areas to be treated with great sensitivity, especially in a group situation. The subject of death involves one of the deepest of all human emotions and it should no longer be a forbidden subject as far as children are concerned and should be accepted as an inevitable part of life.

Feelings of loss: The following questions for discussion are in no way meant to be substitutes for the intimacy of comfort for deep loss on a one-to-one basis, but they might help to pave the way towards acceptance of it.

Loss: Did you ever lose something that you were really fond of? How did you feel if you found it? How did you feel when you didn't? Have you ever been lost at a fair or festival? What could you do? How did you feel when you found your parents? Have you had a pet that died or do you know someone whose pet died? How did you/they feel? What helped? Tell your story to the small group if you feel like it.

Dealing with Anger

Probably the most powerful negative emotion is anger and its control is something we can struggle with all of our lives. Yet nowhere is there more need for adults to give a good example. Since we are all human, this is bound to happen at least occasionally and if we apologise, children are always ready to forgive, which is a trait that we could well emulate.

Relevant to the control of anger, and in fact self-control in general, is a well-known experiment with four year olds. The children were given the choice of having two marshmallows if they waited fifteen minutes or one straight away; about two thirds of them could not wait. In a similar experiment they had to wait only five minutes, but the results were the same.

The follow-up after fourteen years was significant: those who had resisted temptation were more self-confident and more socially competent, with a whole list of desirable attributes, whereas those who had opted for immediate pleasure tended to overreact to irritations and more often provoked arguments and fights.

So parents can be forewarned. This test has been described as the eternal battle between impulse and restraint. Starting at an early age we need to reinforce the advantages of having some control over our negative emotions, and, especially in the present climate, control over our endless desires.

Think of a time when you were really angry. What did you do? What could you have done? Brainstorm ideas: e.g. count to ten; do some deep breathing; talk it over; take time to cool off by yourself; express calmly why you are angry, etc.

Expressing anger. List anger words: e.g. furious, mad, annoyed, irritated, frustrated. Make up sentences to express your anger: 'I feel mad at you when you take my … without asking'.

A creative approach to anger. Paint a picture showing anger. What colour would the anger be? Make a clay or plasticine model of someone being angry; in a small group make a tableau of an angry scene, in turns modelling the different 'statues'; role play a scenario involving anger invented by the group (with rules of no physical or verbal abuse) and rehearsing different ways of calming the situation.

Visualisation: When you are angry try to turn your mind towards a completely different scenario: you could imagine something really funny, or when you had a great time – on holiday, in sport, kicking a goal or having your favourite meal. This is easier if you can distance yourself from the scene of the trouble.

Building a Good Self-Concept

Identity: In pairs find out as much as possible about your partner: their favourite colour, flower, food, hobby, etc. or make a mobile with pictures of your tastes and achievements.

My success book: Make a book of your achievements with your own illustrations or photographs of the best things that you have ever done: it could be learning to swim or ride a bike, or to read, or your first poem. Non writers can make drawings with adults writing in the titles. In a classroom this can take the form of an 'I can' tree, with children's achievements hanging from the branches; at home it can be a mobile with similar messages.

My name is special: Tell what you know about your name. Give yourself another name that you would like to have as well. Choose a nice adjective to go with your name: e.g. Smiling Susan, Jolly John.

Silhouettes and profiles: Lie on wallpaper with arms slightly outstretched so that your body can be traced by a partner; cut out and hang temporarily on the wall so that everyone can fix an affirming message with yellow stickers. Alternatively, a picture or photograph of each child can be stuck on to the middle of a sheet of A4 and affirmations written or dictated around it. Profiles of portraits can be made by using an overhead projector and tracing the shadows cast and used for affirmations in the same way.

Affirmations: Write your name at the bottom of a piece of paper, which is then handed round for each of the others to write something nice about you, fold it over and pass it on to the next person to do the same. If this is done in a circle it will come back to the owner, who can read it out to the rest.

Put-ups and put-downs: Think of a time when someone made you feel really good and either draw a picture of it or recount it to a partner. Now do the same when you felt put down by somebody. It is good to share and discuss these experiences *if* agreed.

I Am Loveable And Capable (IALAC): This affirmation is taken from 'A Manual of Non-Violence' (1983). It can be a sort of mantra as it stands for 'I am lovable and capable', sometimes preceded by 'No matter what anyone says'. This has proved to be a helpful confidence restorer and is appropriate for adults and children alike.

What are you good *at?* Name three things that you feel you are good at. Say them first modestly but sincerely and then repeat them in a bragging way. This will help people to acknowledge their merits without appearing to boast about them.

Dressing up to be grand: Young children love to dress up, in fact most of us do. Everyone can make a gold crown and be royal; dressing up boxes in the home or nursery can contain prince and princess outfits, simply adapted from curtains – lace or velvet with props – feathers, wands, etc. Stories from Grimm can be enacted which contain the message of the least powerful being successful in the end. At the fairy tale stage, playing at royalty is not a political issue!

Count your blessings: This can be a group brainstorm or a bedtime reflection; think of all the nice things that have happened to you during the day. It does promote peaceful sleep.

Affirmation Game: At the end of Circle Time take turns in asking someone to change places by saying something nice about them.

Being chosen or rejected: In small groups think of new ways in which to choose teams instead of having leaders who choose in turn. Have you ever been the last one to be chosen? Ideas could include division according to their name in the alphabet or counting numbers which then form the group or team.

First day at school: Everyone joins in acting how they feel; infants could act out the nursery and juniors the infant school. Do you approach someone or stand by yourself? What could the teacher do to make you feel happier?

Relationships

The road to happiness is getting on with each other and this has to start in the early years in the family and then the nursery school. Soon children's play becomes social and they have to learn to give and take and to curb their negative emotions, not by repressing them but being open about what they are feeling. At first the openness is spontaneous and the curbing is difficult, but by the time they are five or six they are more likely to be diffident about saying what they are feeling. Children need a lot of help and support during these stages, especially understanding from adults when they find it hard to control their rage, and ways in which to deal with it to enable them to function socially.

Friendship: What do you like about your friends? What is your idea of a good friend? What makes you quarrel with your friends? How can you help someone who seems lonely or unhappy? What are some of the ways in which you could make friends with someone? How can you join a group with whom you would like to play? These are some of the questions that could be put in Circle Time and get a summary of the answers.

Being friendly: Think of someone you like and describe good things about them to a partner. Have a regular school time when you go and make friends with someone you don't regularly talk to. Say something kind to someone every day. Each child is given the name of a secret 'buddy' who keeps an eye on her/him and is ready to help if necessary. The buddy is not told, but will probably guess.

Feeling left out of it: Your best friend has rejected you. Act out what you could do – be nice to her and try to make up; find another friend but be still friendly to her; ask her why she has treated you like this; explain yourself if you feel you have been misunderstood.

Belonging to the group: Act out a scenario where you want to join in with a group. Should you ask straight away or wait and watch and then ask?

Let me in! In small groups make a closed circle by linking arms and leaving one person outside who has to ask to be allowed in. The rule is that the first two times she is refused and the third time the person asked welcomes her. There should be no forcing on the part of the outsider and this activity can be quite stressful if she is not accepted fairly quickly. The discussion that follows can bring up painful memories of feeling discarded and arouse empathy on the part of those making the closed circle.

It is worth reiterating that children's feelings are to be treated with the utmost respect; we need to be fully aware of their sensitivities. The skills of the facilitator are continually called upon to establish a climate of confident security and to ensure that children should never feel under pressure to reveal their innermost feelings.

Chapter II

The Art and Skills of Good Communication

*'Perhaps what one wants to say is formed in childhood
and the rest of one's life is spent trying to say it?'*
Barbara Hepworth, Sculptor.

The whole emphasis of this book is on dialogue, and the tools for
thoughtful dialogue are clear self-expression and active listening.
There is now a growing movement to explore more deeply the
value of discourse: discussion and dialogue between children and
between children and adults. It has followed naturally from the
realisation of the enormous importance of the role of emotional
literacy in every child's development. This is a confirmation of
the intrinsic connection between the affective and the cognitive
functioning of the mind and the strengthening of this thinking/
feeling link is best supplied by dialogue: talking together in ways

19

that allow individuals to understand the thoughts, feelings and values of each other and thereby to develop inner confidence.

It is undoubtedly the parents who have the first access to real dialogue with their children, and recent research on child development can reinforce our natural instincts to talk a lot to them. This is especially true with regard to the early years. It is worth reiterating for parents like me, who might feel that they have missed out at that stage, that it is never too late and any knowledge about what has been and is going on in our children's minds is always helpful.

In any case, we have always been aware of our babies' needs for attention and love. Nevertheless, most of us have not realised how much social behaviour is being manifested in the first few minutes and hours immediately after birth and during the weeks and months that follow. Of course, we know that babies recognise and prefer their mother's voice from the moment they are born, but their imitation of their fathers' or other carers' gestures (including poking out the tongue!) at just fifteen minutes old, can be more of a surprise.

After a week they bond to their new home environment and soon become distressed when taken somewhere new, and communication with their family plays an increasing role in the dynamics of the relationships. We now have a much better understanding of the extent to which babies have the ability to communicate; they certainly know a good deal more than we give them credit for and it must be very frustrating for them not to be able to convey what they need to say.

Later, when they are learning to speak, there is a constant process of asking questions about the world around them; and their feelings, whether of wonder or frustration, are linked intrinsically to their insatiable need to talk. Our encouragement to express themselves and our ability to listen to them gives great strength to their sense of identity and self-concept.

This brings us to one of the main pivots in the art of communication: the ability to listen deeply, giving all of your attention. So often children feel that they are not really listened to, and frequently they are right; busy parents and teachers have many things on their minds and much work to attend to, so it is really hard to concentrate fully on what is being attempted to communicate.

The Value of Dialogue

Dialogue can be different from ordinary conversation; it can enable both children and adults to develop an appreciation of their inner resources by sharing their thoughts and ideas with others. It has been defined as 'the mutual development of understanding through shared enquiry into the perspectives of others'. One essential feature, therefore, is listening to the other point of view and this certainly engages children and young people emotionally, at the same time as stimulating their thinking. One project for promoting dialogue has been launched in schools in over thirty countries and the conclusion is that 'motivating pupils and teaching them how to learn in this way is far more important than the inculcation of any particular content or set of skills'.

These aims might seem too advanced for younger children, but they can still recall the many unanswered questions that linger on, and they can be relatively free from the inhibitions that can come in adolescence, their natural curiosity and tendency to ask questions providing easy access to the pursuit of real dialogue. An organisation called 'Sapere' is having great success in introducing this use of dialogue under the heading of 'Philosophy for Children', which groups young children into communities of enquiry to identify questions of common interest or concern. These are then pursued in a collaborative spirit: dialogues that respond to the feelings and views of those taking part. This approach encompasses relationships, playfulness, strategic reflection and the ability to make connections; for example, they can have an exciting discussion on 'What is a Monster?'

A good beginning can be made with parents and their young children around stories or a special video, probably on a one-to-one basis, as siblings might be too diverse in their development. We need to bear in mind that quite young children find difficulty in distinguishing fantasy from reality, and the discourse can connect with their imaginative powers at the same time as relating to their own needs and troubles. The rule of treating them as equal partners in discussion and never putting them down or making fun of their notions will ensure their sense of security and trust. The tradition of discussion in the family could be kept alive at mealtimes without too much formality when the children are older.

All children need a lot of practice in taking part in a group discussion. At first it is easier to talk in pairs and then, as they get more used to dealing with other viewpoints and the give and take of a dialogue, they can increase the number of participants. It is a gradual progression towards being able to speak freely without being criticized and to listen without being anxious; and what is more difficult – to learn from the encounter between ideas that they do not immediately agree with.

The teacher or the facilitator plays a considerable role in initiating worthwhile discussion and guiding it on the right lines, away from too much disparate talk and at the same time letting the discussion flow without too much steering. One way of keeping to the subject is to encourage contributions that are related to the previous comment. Children should have the opportunity to carry a self-evaluation of which skills in discussion they have developed well and which they need to work on.

At last dialogue is given its rightful place in the National Curriculum. For the relatively new subject of Citizenship the Qualification Curriculum Authority (QCA) in England recommends all sorts of discussion, whether in the time allotted for PSHE (Personal, Social, Health Education and Citizenship) or in any other lessons. It is now being recognised that one of the best ways of learning is through talking about the subject in question, whether in the literacy hour or in any other area of knowledge. The QCA recommends work in pairs and groups, debates on controversial issues and on school discipline and even a degree of self-government in the practice of democracy. Teachers have found that this purposeful discussion is well worthwhile and it can transform and enrich the life of both the classroom and the home. The results can be an improvement in positive relationships as well as a reduction in playground incidents, and increased tolerance in the classroom. All the skills of affirmation, trust, sharing of one's feelings and communicating can be practised in the secure environment.

With the enormous pressure exerted by the domination of skills' practice, examinations and the league tables, teachers may well feel that there simply isn't enough time to indulge in discussion that is not immediately related to the demands of the National Curriculum, but this is now part of the official curriculum as laid down by the QCA: to take part in discussions with one other person, in small groups and with the whole class; also to research, discuss and debate topical issues, problems and events. These activities should not be confined to the very limited slots provided for Citizenship, but be part of every aspect of the curriculum, and could well be continued in the home.

Circle Time

In a growing number of primary schools Circle Time has become the pivot of classroom life; it has even begun to take hold in secondary classes. It has been called the Magic Circle and can gradually transform the whole atmosphere of the school. Before the establishment of Circle Time, school children had little opportunity of talking about themselves and their feelings and being listened to with respect. For families, the equivalent of Circle Time is probably meal times, as long as the lure of television is kept at bay.

Ever since the earliest traces of humanity circles have played a sustaining role in both the physical and spiritual life of the community, with talk, songs, dances and rituals. That role is more vital than ever with the speed-up of lifestyles and the temptations of rival distractions. By its very nature Circle Time is democratic with no hierarchies and the fact that everyone can have direct eye contact makes for an atmosphere of openness and respect.

Everyone is acquainted with the three golden rules: participants can only speak when they have the magic object in their hands, which might be a beautiful conch shell, a wand or similar treasure. They can pass it on if they have nothing to say at that moment and there should never be any 'put downs', but perhaps the most important aspect of Circle Time is that it embodies the fundamental right of everyone to have their say, which is the essence of democracy. This can be reaffirmed by each child having two badges with 'Right to speak' on them; after using up their two turns they cannot speak again, only listen. After each contribution there can be a short silence so that the children can take in what they have just listened to.

Originally the purpose of Circle Time was to give children the opportunity to speak about themselves, their activities and interests, but now, in many cases, it is being extended to include discussion of their needs and problems, with a view to some sort of consensus and concerted action. Of course, this process does not happen spontaneously; it entails the guidance of sensitive adult facilitators and the introduction of a number of skills such as good communication, active listening, problem solving and group cooperation. There is little doubt that there are large untapped resources in all children which respond positively to this approach. The atmosphere created has to be secure enough for them to trust the group before they share their feelings and emotions. As we have already seen, there has been a big breakthrough in the understanding of the process of learning in the recognition of the enormous influence of the emotions, and Circle Time is the ideal environment for the nurturing of emotional literacy.

Thus, the magic circle can gradually embrace a wider concept than individuals' items of news while keeping it as a starting point. The discussion can then emerge into a series of sensitive issues challenging their moral judgements and value systems, and can be the means by which the essential ingredients that make up the ethos of a school can be consolidated, including self-regulation in behavioural matters and a consistent policy of peaceful conflict resolution.

At its best Circle Time can address the key interpersonal and organisational issues affecting the whole development of the school. Children can learn to have responsibility for solving their own and other people's problems and it is a good opportunity for adults to model positive behaviour.

Teachers who have regularly practised the full use of Circle Time affirm that the sessions are always enjoyable, levels of aggression are lowered and the children feel more free to challenge each other about controversial issues in a blame-free, safe atmosphere. They become more patient with less articulate members and those who are facing difficulties can feel more connected to their classmates. The adults, too, have a higher sensitivity to children's and adult's needs, and conditions are created to put forward new ideas and innovative practices, with the children more willing to take risks, solve problems and support each other's learning.

The fact that parents can be invited and that an extra chair can be placed to welcome an unexpected guest makes a strong link between the school and the home; some of the discussion that has taken place is then more likely to continue in the family.

Modern life presents huge challenges to the natural, full heritage of childhood. Our lives are continually changing but it can be argued that not only is Circle Time essential for the well-being of every student but also a firm foundation for the learning process.

Body Language

The importance of body language has not been given sufficient acknowledgement, although it is estimated that 80 per cent of communication is through facial expressions and the whole stance of the body.

Empathy expressed through body language: Following on from the activity: *Feelings expressed through body language,* half the group can act stressful, miserable, shocked, etc. according to which emotion the facilitator calls out and the other half comfort them without speaking or touching; then they change over.

Assertiveness practised through body language: With the same set up as above, but this time with the whole group at first. They are all asked to walk round assertively with regard to eye contact, posture, facial expression, breathing, gestures, etc. Then they do the opposite: being timid, self-effacing, downcast, slouching, etc. Now half the group goes round assertively and the other half non-assertively, and they indulge in non-verbal communication. Then they change roles. In the discussion that follows: was there a tendency for the assertive ones to become overbearing and bossy? How did the non-assertives feel about that? Finally, half the group are assigned to be aggressive and the other half assertive, with a change over of roles. This exercise brings out the subtle differences between the two approaches and calls for sensitive acting. Did the assertives find their power diminished in a confrontation with a really aggressive person? The rules of no touching and no sounds, as well as no speaking, are especially important in this phase. This activity is a good preparation for dealing with conflict and bullying.

Listening Skills

Creative listening is a matter of attending with your whole being and really concentrating 100 per cent on what you are hearing.

Listening to sounds: Be quite quiet and note any sounds that you can hear. Focus first on those around you and then on those further away. This can be a way to get children to calm down.

Listening to nature: Go outside and choose a place to listen to the sounds of nature: birds, animals, the wind in the trees, buzzing of bees, etc. What other sounds might there be? aeroplanes, cars, tractors, people talking, children playing? What do you most like to listen to? a bird singing, water flowing in a stream?

Rules for good listening: Brainstorm either in pairs or with the whole class: first, rules for good listening, and then rules for bad listening. The list for good listening would include appropriate body language: e.g. encouragement: nods, sympathetic facial expression, pleasant gestures, physical contact where appropriate, such as a hand on the other's shoulder; empathising tone and words, sitting face to face. The rules for bad listeners would include: unsympathetic body language such as no eye contact, criticism, untimely advice, domination, capping, distraction and general lack of encouragement and interest.

Active listening: In groups of two or three, one describes an exciting or a frightening incident and the listener pays no attention; no eye contact, restless, looks at something else which appears to be more interesting, etc. Then a repeat performance with complete attention: eye contact (probably the most important), intense interest shown following every word. Discuss the different feelings of the narrator. Then the roles are reversed. If there is a third person they will take on the observer role and comment on other points the pair might have missed. This is also a useful exercise in detailed observation.

This formula can be used for any subject that the participants choose, for example, each one in turn talking for one minute on something they really enjoy: their hobby, birthday, pet, holiday 'What I like/dislike about school,' etc. and the partner could repeat it in the first person, which is also good listening practice.

A non-listener takes over your story: This is best illustrated by an adult in the first instance: You are asked to describe something that was quite upsetting for you: an accident, your pet was ill, someone called you names. The so-called listener soon takes over and caps what you have just said with a much more traumatic incident that she has experienced. Older children could have fun in 'capping' in pairs with their own imagined incidents.

Promoting Clear Expression

Describe and draw: In pairs one has a simple picture, preferably without people, and describes it accurately to the partner without disclosing its identity; the partner draws it. For example, a circle at the top of the page, a wiggly line half way down across the page, below it a straight line across and below it different squares. A landscape? Alternatively, an object such as a box or pencil could be described and drawn. How accurate was the drawing?

Directions: In pairs one tells the other how to get to other parts of the school: to the hall or the dining room. They can progress with directions as to how to get to various places from the school or from their home. Were the directions accurate? If appropriate they could be tested indoors. For older children this exercise could be extended to 'telephoning' directions as to how to get to a particular place from their school or home, using old mobiles.

Telephoning: In pairs using old mobiles or telephones have an imaginary conversation. For example, invite your partner to your birthday party or to a picnic; ask them to come and play at your house.

Picture match: Cut a number of pictorial cards in half and get each child to take one. They then memorise what is on their half and try to find the owner of the other half, who has also memorised theirs; this must be by means of description only. For a simple example: each half of the cards has a footballer, one trying to score a goal the other the goalie. This activity needs to be in fairly small groups, otherwise it will be too noisy. For older children the cards could be cut into three with a similar procedure.

Interviews: In small groups each one chooses an object that is very special to them and in turn is questioned about it 'Why is it special? What is it like?' etc. An alternative is to go out into the grounds and find something in nature which you especially like (if a flower, do not pick it, but do a drawing instead and colour it when indoors.)

Discussion and Dialogue

All children need a lot of practice in taking part in a discussion. At first it is easier to talk in pairs and then, as they get more used to dealing with other viewpoints and the give-and-take of a dialogue, they can increase the number of participants. It is a gradual progression towards being able to speak freely without being criticised and to listen without being anxious, and what is more difficult, to learn from the encounter with ideas that they do not immediately agree with.

The facilitator plays a considerable role in initiating worthwhile discussion and guiding it on the right lines, away from too much disparate talk, and at the same time letting the discussion flow without too much steering. One way of keeping to the subject is to encourage contributions that are related to the previous comment.

Group discussion subjects: The groups should be of a reasonable size, if possible not more than eight in each so that everyone has the chance to participate. Subjects could include: 'Are exams necessary?'; 'Should children watch television for more than two hours a day?' There could be debates on these subjects with a proposer and seconder on each side. This will be a sound preparation for discussions later on about the needs of the community.

Discussions on school rules and behaviour. When the children are more familiar with discussion, they can turn their attention to the running of their class, and, later, the school. Teachers can raise questions about their own needs: for example, what can be done about the excessive noise in the classroom? Calling out? Everyone wanting the teacher's help at the same time? How can the dinner queue be managed sensibly? Good ideas do come from the children when they are consulted: one good idea that came from them was to ease the pressure on the teacher by asking one of the other pupils what they wanted to know and then only if necessary to ask the teacher.

Rotating Circles: Two circles of the same number of chairs facing each other. A topic is given for the pairs opposite each other to discuss for one minute; then the outer circle children move to the next chair clockwise and have the same discussion with their new partner. Topics can vary, from their preferences to their opinions on a character in a book they are all reading, or an experience of being made fun of or being put down.

Character roleplay in group discussion: In groups of four or five, a card is distributed to each member, who has to keep it secret. First time round they are all given different aspects of the role of a character who is unhelpful: for example, the one who always interrupts; the one who has objections to every idea put forward; the one who wants to talk about his own experiences all the time; the silent one who shows disapproval non-verbally; the joker. After discussion, give out a second series of cards, this time with positively helpful characters. What differences were there in the way the two discussions went?

31

Ranking: Prepare nine different statements about a familiar subject and, in pairs, agree to put them in order of importance, so number 1 is the most and number 9 the least. For example, there could be nine statements about the importance of good listening and they might agree that the most important was not to criticize and the least was not to fidget. They might decide that all nine of the statements were equally important and therefore end up with a straight line. The general practice with this activity is to go for a diamond shaped conclusion: in rows, one at the top, two equal, three equal, two equal and one at the bottom. Older children could join up with another pair and see if they can agree amongst the four of them the order of importance. This is a real test of seeing the other person's point of view. For young children they might just agree about the order of two or three statements such as: 'It's better to have school uniforms'; 'It's better to have school dinner than a packed lunch'; 'It's better to make your own school rules'.

Listing skills needed in discussion groups: Brainstorm the various skills needed: for example, listening, taking turns, responding, participating, concentrating, standing up for what you believe, questioning, thinking, cooperating, asking other people's opinions, collaborating, etc. The list would be added to as they become more practiced.

Communication: In conclusion, there is one essential element in the art and skills of communication, and that is the ability to reflect on what you have listened to and what you have discussed. Time spend in reflection is often at a premium, but it is probably the most valuable part of the whole learning process and should have its rightful place in all aspects of education.

Chapter III

The Importance of Creativity and Play

'Like the new moon thy life appears;
A little strip of silver light,
And widening outward into night
The shadowy disk of future years;
And yet upon its outer rim,
A luminous circle, faint and dim,
And scarcely visible to us here,
Rounds and completes the perfect sphere;'
from 'To a Child' by Henry Wadsworth Longfellow

Play and Creativity: The Birthright of Childhood

Childhood is the very life blood of humanity; it is the true foundation on which the adult is built. By its very nature it is based on the child making sense of the world through creative

play, and we interfere with that nature at their peril, whether as caring adults or from the pressures of modern society. Right from the early years they know instinctively how to explore every aspect of their development. Certainly they need an environment where they can be free to play, using all their senses and their burgeoning imagination as they progress towards participation with their peers.

As parents and teachers all we have to do is to provide the basics for this stage: water, air, earth and utensils to manipulate these elements, and also very simple toys so that as much is left to the imagination as possible. It is tempting for adults to spy on their children as they act out their observations of our behaviour with deadly accuracy, or to make a peep-show of their soaring flights of fantasy. One of my very earliest recollections was to hear the suppressed laughter of the grown-ups as they listened with the door slightly ajar to my animated diatribe to my motley collection of toy animals. I dried up in mid sentence! The privacy and independence of children's make-believe is sacred.

The sheer beauty of these stretches of the imagination is to pave the way to a creative spirit, which can stand us in good stead for the rest of our lives and is the passport to a good self-concept. Einstein continually emphasized the fact that the secret of happ-iness was in the imagination and that it was the magic of fairy stories that could be a great source of happiness; he was convinced that the power of the imagination had influenced him far more than any of his intellectual studies.

It is this creative side that can be neglected in young children's schooling today: the great emphasis on the so-called 'basics' can drive nursery teachers to organise their pupils' play into pur-poseful directions towards numeracy and literacy. At the same time their free time can be over controlled by parents in their concern for their children's progress. The news today featured a complaint from the Inspectorate that parents were not doing enough to prepare their five-year-olds (and more often four-year-olds) for the beginning of schooling. We all know that our 'competitors' in the rest of Europe only start compulsory edu-cation at the age of six or often seven, when children sail through the accomplishment of these skills, while having had much more time for a rounded education in the nursery schools. This means that in their explorations young children can grasp a feel for the magic of numbers and letters and the fascination of books long before they study them formally.

Inseparable from the fantasies and the imagination of creative play is the growth of the spoken word; at first in monologue form and then a running commentary which takes note of other children playing alongside them. Soon dialogue begins in ear-nest, and the more they have the opportunity to play with others the better their ability to communicate. Closely linked to talking together is the impact on their social development; they learn to give and take and share, which is a big hurdle for the very young.

Later, when they develop their own games they will make the rules, which can be quite complicated, as anyone who has tried to penetrate the complexities of games of marbles or conkers knows only too well.

Much of the organising and rule making is initiated by drama which has its origins in the imitation of what is going on around them and soon develops into farfetched scenarios of imaginative action, acted alongside the more structured games. Here roles can be negotiated and leadership experienced, building up a microcosm of the structure of their society. These days of creative childhood provide the backbone of what it takes to become a good citizen: a good concept of one's own uniqueness and the experience of positive relationships with one's peers. Now external influences are putting at risk this essential stage in their development, so it is more important than ever to give them the full benefit of a joyful and creative childhood which will stand them in good stead for the rest of their lives.

What we can do

Having stressed that adults should not interfere with spontaneous play, the following ideas might be helpful in stimulating children's independent creativity.

Play with the elements
Water: In the kitchen sink, water trough or paddling pool with a range of utensils, sieves, measuring jugs, etc.; floating home-made boats; exploring puddles, ponds, streams and the sea.
Earth: Play with mud; make things out of playdough, plasticine or clay: for example, small animals, pots, scenes of people; sand – dry and wet, castles and buildings not only at the seaside.
Air: Make, decorate and fly kites; fly balloons, banners, flags, windsocks; blowing bubbles, especially the soapy water kind.
Painting and printing: leaf, vegetable, hand and string painting; fabric printing, wax resist, blow painting; blob, fold and cut out, for example, a butterfly.
Collages: Various materials such as lace, buttons, coloured tissue paper and foil can be pasted or glued to make a picture or illustration of an event. This can also be done in pairs taking alternate turns.
Sense stimulations: Feeling different textures; try out a range of smells: flowers, herbs, food, blindfold and guess what they are; do the same with sounds: 'musical instruments'; bird song, outside and indoor ones: taste a number of different flavours and have a similar guessing game, look at bright colours in nature or in the home and paint a colourful picture. Feely bag stories using a bag full of objects handed round for the listeners to feel as the storyteller proceeds.
Memory: Kim's game with variations of adding and removing objects.
Music: Home-made percussion bands enhance children's love

of rhythm. Expose children to the widest possible variations of music, including worldwide songs and instruments; music can stir our innermost feelings, it can help us relax, and according to research soothing music can actually improve memory and behaviour, whereas aggressive music has the opposite effect.

Dance and movement: Besides formal sessions it feels good to dance spontaneously to music, even for a short time.

Toys: Give simple toys and encourage them to make their own: for example, a doll in the Rudolph Steiner tradition can be very easily made by folding a square of cloth with a little stuffing for the head.

Worry dolls: These are small figures, preferably home-made, to which children can tell all their troubles at bedtime. In the morning, after a night under the pillow, the doll has wished all the worries away. This practice, I am told, originated in South America.

Puppets: These can be made out of mittens, socks or just paper bags, although older children could make papier maché heads on a cardboard tube and glue beautiful fabric to them. As with all toys it is the activity that one does with them that is important rather than any finished result. As shown in the rest of this book, there are endless possibilities of enacting scenarios and if the puppet is in the maker's own image, it can be used to express feelings and speech without embarrassment.

It is good to remember that if children are given too many toys, especially mechanical ones, they can easily become overwhelmed and cannot concentrate on any one toy for long; likewise toys that fulfil all functions and leave nothing for the children to achieve are soon discarded, however impressive they are.

Stories: Tell and read as many varied stories for young children as possible, including ones dealing with feelings, fantasies and adventure. Encourage them to make up their own stories, perhaps

starting with a group one, with everyone adding a sentence, or even a word, in turn. It is wise to try to avoid the usual television themes of violence, otherwise they will rely on them rather than give full play to their own powers of imagination; or they could discuss an alternative nonviolent ending. You could, perhaps, encourage them by including some outrageous but nonviolent themes in your own contributions, letting them know that the sky's the limit in the fantasy world.

Books to lose oneself in: It is a wonderful moment when you can curl up with a favourite book and actually live the adventures that transpire. It is quite different from watching passively a film or a television programme. Although you have not written the story, you can be so immersed that you are really a part of the action and released from everyday life in a creative way, and it may even spark off stories of your own.

This delight is founded on the inspiration of parents reading to their children and choosing exciting books to look at from babyhood onwards. There can be a follow up at school, where reading for sheer pleasure can take the place of analysis of texts, correct punctuation and spelling, which can then be relegated to their proper place at a later stage when the enjoyment has been well established.

Poetry: Children can be natural poets: if they are encouraged to write their own poems, using all their senses and feelings, they can produce little gems. There are now various community projects such as poetry readings and recitations for all ages, often organised for Poetry Day – October 9th. These sessions have helped to supplement poetry learning in the schools, which has been rather neglected.

Poetry that you learn when young can stay with you all your life; its rhythm and sheer flow of words appeals to children, especially poems with a sense of fun and humour – and they don't have to rhyme.

An Affinity with Nature

'Children's voice in the orchard
Between the blossom and the fruit-time.'
from 'Landscapes' by T.S. Eliot

There has always been a strong link between creativity and nature. From a very early age children are fascinated with the natural world, and this is the time to support and nourish their interest. Even the most caring parents find it difficult not to hurry their small offspring as they want to spend endless time in examining in great detail some little creepy crawly they have spotted on a wall or in someone's garden.

By the time they get to school this affinity might have worn a bit thin, partly because of everybody's busy life. However, what the parents begin, the teachers can continue: whether it is having a small plot of one's own, a container or a window box if there is little space, or a class garden to be cultivated in the school grounds. It is well known that such plots are seldom vandalised, and if this does happen all heaven is let loose: a good example of children's innate sense of justice.

Again, it is not too early to begin to teach them to look after the planet: treasuring wild flowers with a wildlife area, however small; providing nest boxes and shelters for birds and creatures whose habitat has been depleted. At school they can learn about the various disappearing species and the need to conserve the rainforest. We have to tread a fine line between enthusing them with the need to protect the earth and dwelling on the consequences of what is happening: for example, the depletion of the ozone layer and the risk of disastrous climate change.

My garden: If I had a garden what would it be like? What would I grow and how would I make it flourish? What does a garden need? What animals, birds and insects, etc. would be in my garden? A pond? A wild life bit? They could paint a picture of their ideal garden or have a group collage. Then facing reality, what

can you have either at home or at school? It might be only a window box or hanging basket or a large container, but this could be planned and started with seeds, helping them make connections with growth, which is so often missing when buying ready flowering plants.

An animal of my choice: Choose an animal and then imagine that you are that animal. Where do you live and how are you cared for? What are your needs and do others, animals or humans, understand them? Not everyone is allowed a pet, but school classes often have one for which they assume full responsibility.

Adopt a tree: This can follow the ideas suggested for an animal. It is your special tree and you can give it a hug (unless it's prickly!). This happened to me when I was led blindfold by an innocent young 'guide' who had decided my choice for me!

Making sense of the garden: Go out into the garden or grounds, or the woods, together with adults and choose something that illustrates the five senses: the perfume of herbs, bird song, buzzing of bees, gaudy flowers, the touch of pebbles. Carry the sensations in your head and talk about them.

Choose a treasure from nature: Some treasures you can bring back, like a beautiful stone, autumn leaves or an intricate seed; if your treasure is a flower then draw and colour it. Say why you feel that your choice is so precious.

Creating an atmosphere of peace and tranquility: We all need spaces of quiet and tranquility and children especially require considerable time to assimilate all that is happening to them as they are rapidly learning about the world. Most adults working professionally give themselves a ten minute break every hour and that should set a good example to teachers, who definitely need that respite; they don't need to worry about the National Curriculum being short changed; it is well established that learning will be of a higher quality after reflection.

This break should be as welcome in the home as at school; it might be regularly after a meal or at bedtime, or after one lesson, both morning and afternoon, in the classroom. What to do with the ten minutes? Children could just be quiet, closing their eyes, and it is interesting how many of them are pleased to have this space. They might just watch their breathing, which is often what people do when they are meditating; or they might watch thoughts and feelings that come to mind. This might be especially appropriate if they have been feeling angry and need to calm down. In the classroom situation many children look forward to this break from continual noise and stress, and they have been known to play a part in hushing the inevitable disrupters.

A Haven of peace: Have a quiet place which is specially allocated for those who want some peace and quiet in the home or school. Space could be a problem so it might have to be just a quiet corner of a room which is less noisy than the rest. All children love some kind of cubby hole: it could be an old tent in the summer or an 'igloo' under the table.

A magic spot in nature: Choose a place where you want to be and just relax or listen to the sounds around you. A lovely experience is to lie on the grass or woodland and gaze up at the clouds rolling by or the tree trunks soaring above.

Guided Fantasies: We are fortunate that our imagination can take us on fabulous journeys without stirring from the home or the classroom; all children enjoy a story and this is their story and their exploration of something that is very special to them. In the first instance the teacher or parent weaves the fantasy and later it can be the turn of the children. Themes vary from mysterious paths through the woods to their own little cottage with all their treasures around them; caves encrusted with rocks or gems of all colours; a space ship to the moon and stars; a magic flying boat that sails across the oceans; a trip to an ideal land on the back of a mythical animal – a unicorn or a beautiful, friendly dragon.

When children have painted what they have been feeling after these fantasies, the results are truly wonderful. This can be an initiation into the wonders of nature for children who have been deprived of the delights of running wild in the countryside.

Yoga for children: Many adults take time out to do yoga and now children are often joining in. Young children are so supple that they find the various postures quite natural and this practice will help to keep them in good trim; the fact that many of the exercises are likened to animals appeals to them and the whole process creates a sense of security and well-being.

There are growing numbers of schools where yoga is taught, mostly as an after school activity, and these are proving to be popular. Children enjoy taking postures in the form of different animals, including birds and fish, and trees are also featured as models. Their imagination is stimulated and their whole body energised, and in the peaceful relaxed atmosphere they respond to breathing properly.

Children who find it difficult to concentrate or who are hyperactive can benefit greatly from this practice; it helps them to control their emotions and to deal with stress. It can also be an antidote to too much sitting at computers or watching television.

There are plenty of good books with simple instructions and also organisations giving details of teachers and classes available, so parents and teachers can get support in an area that maybe unfamiliar to them (see bibliography).

An extra benefit is that this is an activity that can be shared by adults and children in an atmosphere of calm and relaxation.

Chapter IV

Whatever Happened to Childhood?

'The earth provides enough to satisfy man's need, but not everyman's greed.'
Mahatma Gandhi

This millennium is unique in promoting a whole new concept of what it is to be young. It seems that the notion of childhood, with specific needs for the growing child, is being eclipsed in a frenzy to enter into adult life with all possible speed.

Apparently these aspirations are embraced at an ever earlier age and we can explore some of the underlying reasons for this phenomenon, which is creeping up on us. There is little doubt that the overwhelming influence is that of the greed of consumerism, which is increasingly penetrating the home and now the school as never before. Commercial forces are at work aiming at the widest possible age groups, not only at the supermarket checkout, but near, or even in, school playgrounds, distributing free cartons of sugar puffs and fizzy drinks, not to mention free exercise books for the teachers.

On an even more insidious level, children are deliberately targeted for 'pester power', encouraging them to harangue their parents to buy toys, clothes, electronic games and devices such as mobile phones, not to speak of videos, DVDs and hi-fis. This pressure is greatly intensified by the sale of collectibles, which is developed to an unprecedented pitch by linking favourite films and television serials with sweets, comics, T-shirts, toys, designer outfits for dolls and the very latest weapons of destruction for boys.

The overall trend is to encourage children to endlessly acquire possessions, extending marketing to an ever younger age group – an extreme example is a video guaranteed to stimulate babies from the age of three weeks! In his book, *Lost Icons* (2000), Rowan Williams, the Archbishop of Canterbury, makes the point that if the present definition of a child is of a consuming object, then adults who are caring for them should be asking questions about what we take for granted or collude in. He asks, 'what can we say about a marketing culture that so openly feeds children's desires for possessions?' – and the implication is that we should say a great deal!

Here are some of the very latest developments in the marketing field aimed at pre-teenage children: bottled water companies who are competing to persuade primary school children to add their brand of mineral water to their fizzy drinks, on the basis that this will be beneficial. For the affluent, sales of designer clothes for children from as young as two years old have leapt up by almost 25 per cent in the last five years, with some items costing more than £1,000! Food designers are becoming even more adept at exploiting children's fascination for new products: for example,

Heinz have introduced a new colour, orange, to entice them. The influence that British children have on their parents' spending power has now been estimated to be worth about £30 billion!

In such a competitive society this imperative to accumulate cannot be separated from the pressure for children to keep up with the group, whether by acquiring the latest designer trainers or the new Play Station; and the satisfaction of going one better than the rest is an inevitable temptation. Manipulation of the collectibles, the 'tie-ins', by the promoters adds to the tendency to score off one's peers: as for example, when some cards from the Pokomon craze were deliberately 'rarified' to increase the price.

At a deeper and even more worrying level are the messages continually being conveyed to our children: that might is right, both on an individual and a global level, and that violence is an acceptable part of every day life. Television programmes are loaded with acts of terror, brutality and fighting, and as a majority of children now have a television in their bedroom, it is more difficult to supervise their viewing, both before and after 9 p.m. Even more obsessive are the computer games designed to lead on to increasing violence, with what Rowland Williams (2000) describes as 'the conscription of children into the fetishistic hysteria of style wars'.

Just as children model themselves on the adults around them, they are influenced in the same way by the characters in television and computer games programmes, and since the heroes are not usually endowed with the value systems that we would desire for our children, this presents a formidable problem. As this is an era of stardom, football, TV and pop idols, all exert a great influence on their admirers; this can be a positive factor, especially if the stars engage in good works and set a good example. It can also be a salutary lesson on the dangers of hero worship, as when the football star is indicted for a deliberate foul or the TV celebrity is condemned for cheating.

Moreover, the present climate can have a distinctly personalised influence on the young and their own aspirations to become a star, usually in the pop world. It is not just the would-be high flyers who are promoted by ambitious parents towards talent competitions and beauty contests; huge numbers of young hopefuls are waiting to be 'discovered'. This is more of a girls' domain, usually with sexual overtones in postures and dress, with words to match. The general effect may sometimes be considered 'cute' in young children, but it rings false and must inevitably be a source of disillusion and disappointment – even for the few who are the winners. This precocious concept of young girls as sexual objects, fired by show-biz 'glamour' and the appeal of TV ads, makes for a hurried childhood, impatient to get into the 'real' world.

Although there are many youths eager to form a group and get into the charts, boys are more deeply engaged in the latest computer games, often pitting their skills against unseen competitors on the internet. Also both sexes spend considerable time listening to pop music through the latest electronic sound system which can sometimes tend them towards a more solitary existence, with less social contact. This trend, which has been typical of teenagers, is reaching an ever younger age group.

It is significant that in all these areas the stereotypes of predatory male and seductive female are continually exploited, whether in the division of toys: designer dolls or killer missiles; seductive girl performers or stony faced, male pop singers. All this intensifies the pressure on the girl to be a sexual object while endorsing in the boy a macho image.

These relatively new developments in the lifestyle of children add up to a truncated childhood; with TV, the internet and computer games taking over from games, exercise and hobbies.

Of course, this is a general trend and by no means all young children are becoming 'couch potatoes', but the figures show that for many their present way of life constitutes a health risk, not to mention the effects of a diet of too much junk food. This presents an enormous challenge to parents in particular, and also to teachers; there has never been a time when young children are so vulnerable in the hands of their exploiters and it will need all of their parental and teaching skills to safeguard the natural childhood that those in their care deserve.

What we can do

There is a lot that we can do, but in the face of such powerful forces, bent upon taking over our children's lives, we might well feel undermined and impotent. As individuals our efforts might seem minuscule, but together we are strong. I am reminded of the story of the small bird who, when he saw that a gigantic fire was consuming the jungle, took a drop of water in his beak and let it drop on the flames and continued to fly back and forth diligently. The other creatures mocked him but he only said 'I do what I must'. The story has a happy ending: an angel flies by and seeing what the little bird was doing, produced a great rainfall and the fire went out!

This story, taken from 'Living Values', can be used for ideas for original drama, showing the possibilities of changing something if everyone does their bit. There is indeed much that parents and teachers can accomplish; we are together with our young children for the greater part of their time and as a community we do not have to give in to market forces and the materialistic society.

On a more day-to-day level, there is a great case for presenting a joint front with other parents as well as teachers and mutually agreeing on the boundaries that we intend to establish and maintain. In this way we are able to counter the argument that children most often adopt to get their way: namely that all the other parents allow it, whether it is how much television or buying the latest trainers.

Very tentatively I would like to make suggestions on dealing with some of the most salient points raised above, knowing and empathizing with the enormous difficulties that parents and teachers are up against in trying to educate children to become fulfilled and whole human beings.

Firstly, we can spare them some of the endless rush and pressure of everyday life, giving them space to be themselves, as described in the previous chapter on creativity and play. Some years ago David Elkind wrote a book entitled, *The Hurried Child* (1981). This was about the United States, but children are being hurried through their childhood more and more in our country as well. In many cases their aspirations are to be grown up as soon as possible.

Their appetite to possess is inflamed by the constant pressure of consumerism, which promotes everything that can be sold to eager buyers, except that for this age group it is the parents who are expected to fork out. Just as we will not tolerate whining in our offspring, we also have to clamp down on pestering, which is used so openly as an efficient selling device. So perhaps we should make them completely responsible for organising their own pocket money, with no advances on birthday and Christmas presents allowed. (It is tempting for the children to ask for them a year ahead or more and then, when the great day comes, we relent and give extra!) We could certainly enlist the teachers' help in the numeracy programmes in their planning and calculations as to what they can afford. As soon as they are old enough, they could have some indication of the family finances, even if it is only how much pocket money it is reasonable for them to expect.

The development of the electronics industry has penetrated into every household and needs strong boundaries to keep it under control. Rules as to how much television and which programmes can be watched need to be discussed when the children are old enough, and this also goes for computer games, mobile phones and the internet. There is no doubt that there will be strong feelings against any restrictions, but if the order is well established very early on and alternative pursuits and interests cultivated, it is more likely that a consensus will be reached, particularly if some flexibility is allowed.

The issue of violent programmes and computer games must be tackled: if a grown-up can watch the programmes or play computer games with them sometimes, it will be possible to talk about them afterwards: Did they make you afraid? Who was your favourite/less favourite character? Is violence alright as long it is make-believe? (One for the young philosophers!). The usual cartoons for the very young are often full of violence, but there are some delightful DVDs and videos on loan or sale that have a range of suitable stories that they could enjoy instead.

On the question of children modelling themselves on the characters they view and play, it is comforting to remember that they will always act out the roles of superman and the so-called goodies who are inevitably violent and then they will progress to their next model. Although it may seem hard to believe, their adopting of our behaviour will be more lasting and more potent in the long run. They will have to work their own way through this medley of 'stars' blazing before their eyes and we can help by portraying heroes and heroines in stories or real life who have really earned the acclaim.

We also need to keep a close watch on consumerism with regard to the food they are persuaded to want. If children are given a diet of natural foods right from the start, they are much less likely to crave for the junk food and the sugar to which they can soon become addicted, and this could have an impact on their behaviour as well as their health.

Finally, this book is in no way wanting to idealise childhood, nor to be nostalgic about the past. We all know that children are not angels and that they struggle between good and bad just as we all do. We have more understanding of their needs than previous generations and now have greater possibilities of enabling them to realise their full potential, both as individuals and as respected members of the community.

However, we do need to be fully aware of the dangers of the ever present power struggle for our children's minds and aspirations. We need them as allies in a world of endless temptations, and although there has always been a certain amount of natural conflict between the generations, this is a relatively new intervention imposing itself on their childhood.

With our increasing knowledge of our children's natural inclinations and assets, we are set to have a more fulfilled relationship with them and to be able to face the future together with courage. The progress in technology has brought much freedom from ignorance and hardship and there is no question of going back. The advantages in education of computers and the internet are indisputable; and it is up to us as parents and teachers to preserve the balance, both in terms of content and time spent.

Chapter V

Living Values

'You cannot teach a man anything.
You can only help him discover it within himself.'
Galileo Galilei

The ethos of the home and the school is built on a foundation of core values such as cooperation, respect, tolerance, love, responsibility and freedom, and the challenge to parents and teachers alike is how to develop modes of behaviour which encompass them. As ever, the most influential teaching children will receive is our own behaviour: from a very young age they will be constantly imbued with our moral codes and they will be constantly watching us, which is somewhat disconcerting. They will immediately detect any double standards, although they might wait until adolescence to confront us. As Mary Warnock says in her book, *The Intelligent Person's Guide to Ethics* (1998), 'You cannot order children to be moral, but you can teach them and better still show them'.

As we embark on the long process of helping our children to understand our own values and the reasons for them, we can count on them being natural allies, as most children want to be good rather than bad and they definitely want to be happy rather than unhappy. We can explore how we can work on our own moral values by recognising the dignity of the individual child and enhancing each one's self-worth. We now have the great advantage of a more open relationship with our children and are more aware of the great potential that they have to be able to discuss in depth and to begin to think logically; and this is what is needed to sort out their feelings about right and wrong, good and bad with regard to a framework of values.

The value of respect is all-important in our approach to this type of discussion: so children's opinions should be listened to and considered, as will the opinions of their peers, which makes for an interchange of views. The content of any discussion must be appropriate to their age and development, especially as very young children find it difficult to distinguish between degrees of moral conduct. For example, they are liable to judge by quantity or bulk instead of motivation; for example, to break a dozen plates purely by accident could be considered much naughtier than Granny's favourite cup which her grandchild had been told not to touch.

Also, because fantasy plays such a vital role in their lives, it is only gradually that they learn to distinguish between fact and fiction. They often believe that their play is reality and what happens in it is true life; so in engaging in dialogue with them we need all our tact not to undermine their convinced opinions. We can initiate discussions which, while accepting their differing perceptions of morality, can guide them into clearer concepts of right and wrong.

But dialogue cannot be in a moral vacuum and children's sensibilities can be opened up through the telling of stories and the enactment of drama. The advantage of centring the talk round a story rather than concentrating on more personal experience enables the discussion to be more objective. As all young children learn by doing, activities featuring various values such as cooperation, honesty, respect etc., reach home more than any admonitions.

Finally, I believe that the way to live morally is inseparable from the quality of one's life. We need time and space both to care for ourselves and for others. For some families religious belief will reinforce their moral sense; others may designate their own set of values, and it is interesting to see what children will produce when asked to create their own. To be peaceful and have time to reflect could become a luxury in today's world. For children especially, the delights and demands of television and computer games can dominate not only their space, but also their sense of values. Any creative activity can provide a valuable antidote and a short time set aside for a peaceful interlude could consolidate the good experiences they have encountered during the day.

The Living Values Project

The most comprehensive and worthwhile guide to values education is the project, 'Living Values', which is now being taught in over seventy countries worldwide. It is described as a partnership among educators around the world, and is supported by UNESCO, sponsored by the National Committee of UNICEF (Spain) and the Brahma Kumaris, in consultation with the Education Cluster of UNICEF (New York). Its purpose is to provide guiding principles and tools for the development of the whole person, recognising that the individual is comprised of physical, intellectual, emotional and spiritual dimensions.

In order to decide which values they should concentrate on they got people in over sixty countries to list universal values that would be present in a better world, and the twelve most popular were: cooperation, freedom, happiness, honesty, humility, love, peace, respect, responsibility, simplicity, tolerance and unity. It aims to develop these twelve values to fulfil the potential of the individual and create harmonious, effective communities.

The Living Values Education Project provides guidelines in the form of books for teachers of children from 3 to 7, 8 to 14, Young Adults, Parent Groups and teachers of children of refugees and asylum seekers, providing opportunities to experience values through activities – songs, stories, plays, games, music, movement, drama, art, craft, visualisations, discussion and writing. Included in this book are synopses of several of the stories to give a taster of the imaginative content of the activities.

As it is impractical to deal with all of the values cited, and of course there could be many others, this book will take two, cooperation and honesty, and explore the types of experience and activities that could promote them in school and in the home.

Cooperation

Human beings are by their very nature cooperative; we could never have survived if we had not helped each other throughout our long evolution. At present, children are exposed to far more competition than cooperation, although it is evident that they will need the skills to engage with each other and work as a community throughout their lives. Having good relationships is clearly one of the essential requirements for happiness and this is put to the test in the very early years.

There are so many advantages of cooperation: feelings of goodwill towards other people instead of being isolated and left out, no anxiety about having to win or otherwise feeling a failure and getting affirmation and encouragement from others as rivalry diminishes. When there is an atmosphere of cooperation in the classroom it helps to promote good behaviour, as the majority can voice their disapproval of the disruption caused by a minority. Group or individual exercises on cooperation can be particularly potent in carrying out the policy against bullying in the school.

Up to the age of seven, children have difficulty in seeing events from another's perspective. Piaget (1977: 327) calls this transition the period from the morality of constraint to the morality of cooperation; but this transition depends on whether the child has opportunities to practise cooperation and actively construct patterns of thought about these experiences. The following activities seek to give children such opportunities – creating an atmosphere in which violence seems totally out of place and where constructive approaches are modelled.

Cooperative murals: In small groups plan a peaceful landscape; then decide among yourselves who will do the sky, trees, animals, children, etc. Create the picture with coloured pastels on plain sheets of wallpaper. A lot of cooperation will be needed not to get in each other's way. There can be variations on this theme such as doing a picture in pairs, each one taking a turn to add to it. The subject could be agreed beforehand or it could be progressively imaginative. This idea could also be carried out as a joint collage using pictures of people cut out from magazines and sticking them together to make a scene of cooperation.

Musical mural: Play soothing music while a small group paints a wallpaper mural using their imagination. Then when the music stops each student moves to take the place of the one on the right and the last one goes to the beginning. This gives scope for freedom of expression and no one need feel inadequate.

Patchwork paintings: Each child has a small square and paints what comes to mind about the theme chosen by the group. Then they negotiate, either verbally or non-verbally, how to combine them on a sheet large enough to encompass all of the individual squares. Was it easier to agree when you could discuss it or when you had to rely on non-verbal communication?

Collages in pairs: Assemble all sorts of materials for a collage, including small buttons, coloured tissue paper, beautiful cloth and foil. Take turns to add items and if necessary get an adult to stick them on.

Creative collaboration: In groups of not more than three or four plan to build something of their choice: a castle, tower, bridge, statue, boat, church, aeroplane, an animal, etc. Decide what materials to use: newspaper, clay, multi-media?

Blindfold clay sculpture: two children take turns at contributing to the making of a piece of sculpture from a solid lump of clay. They do not talk, but decide mutually when they think it is finished and then they look.

Group Clay Sculpture: each child has a ball of clay or clay-dough the size of a large orange and is told to make three shapes: a ball, a cube and a snake. Then one at a time they place their piece in the centre to make a group sculpture where they feel it is appropriate and with no talking. Discuss and photograph the finished sculpture.

Squiggles: In pairs, the children take turns in adding to a 'squiggle' that can either be started by the adult or one of the children. After a few turns, they stop and agree on a name for the 'squiggle'. The process can be repeated until they have several named 'squiggles'; then they can make up a story using the named pictures in order. Source: Winnicott (1964). This could be in the form of a painting, with each one adding to it in turn.

Group cooperation: In small groups brainstorm incidents where cooperation is needed, for example, a car stuck in the mud, someone fallen in the street, a percussion band. Mime the scenario and let the audience guess what is happening.

Stories of Cooperation

These brief scenarios can be acted out by the children in mime and the audience can guess what the message was about. Scenes of animals acting cooperatively can be a beginning.

Elephants protecting their young: When a predator such as a lion or tiger threatens the herd, elephants place themselves in a circle with the young protected inside and face the attackers, who are intimidated by the threat.

Dolphins saving lives: There are many stories of dolphins who rescue humans in distress. One such is where they actually pushed a shipwrecked sailor on a raft to the safety of the shore.

Cooperative meerkats: Meerkats take turns in being on guard against enemies, sitting on their hind legs bolt upright at the highest vantage point. Those who have no offspring take care of the little ones while their parents hunt for food.

Swimmy: This is one of many stories that feature cooperation. Swimmy is a little fish who, like his friends, is afraid of being eaten by the big fish. He arranges that they all swim in a formation that makes them look like an enormous fish which would frighten their predators away. Small animals such as meerkats use a similar ploy when confronted with young lions; they run close together giving the impression of one enormous beast.

Frogs caught in the cream: Two frogs slipped into a bowl of cream when they were trying to have a drink. Luckily they knew how butter was made so they both paddled frantically until the cream turned to butter and they were able to climb out!

The king and the bunch of sticks: The king had a minister who had three sons who didn't help him; they just went their own way. He asked the king what he could do to teach them to work together, helping him with his many duties. The king told him to get a bundle of sticks and ask which one of them could break it in two. They all tried but failed. At this point the audience could be asked what could be done. The solution shown by the king was

to divide the sticks into three bundles, which were then easy to break in two. Source: *Living Values.*

The King and Queen and their Three Children: The king and queen had one wish for each of their three children. They wished that the first be given great wealth, and that the second should become very famous. After seeing the results of the first two wishes, they wished that the third would be the most loving and giving person in the world. What do you think each one was like? Source: original story by children from West Kidlington School.

Cooperate or starve: At first everyone was starving, although they had plenty of food in narrow-necked jars and long spoons to feed with. What could they do? A small group could be supplied with long bamboo sticks to get 'food' from the narrow-necked jars and try to eat. They will soon solve the problem by feeding each other. If the props are not easily available, they can pretend that their elbows won't bend and so they cannot use a spoon to feed themselves.

Honesty

Stories can be found or invented for any value. This one illustrates the virtue of honesty.

The Emperor and his Seed: This is based on an old Chinese folktale and is my favourite in the repertoire of the 'Living Values' project. It is the story of an Emperor who wanted to find a worthy successor; so he gave everyone a seed and decreed that the person who had produced the most beautiful flowers from it in a year's time would succeed him to the throne.

A small girl called Serena plucked up courage to go, although she was quite poor. When the time came, all the people brought magnificent flowers, but Serena hadn't managed to produce a single shoot, in spite of all of the care she had bestowed on her seed. When the emperor had seen all the offerings, he led Serena to the front and proclaimed her as his successor. Can you guess what his secret was? This is a great story for mime or drama; when we acted it out a tall lad from the Caribbean took the part of little modest Serena!

There is a strong case for treating subjects of high moral value with a pinch of humour, as for example the *Cautionary Tales* of Hilaire Belloc (1995), with Martha who told so many lies. Fables are a great source of moral teaching with a light touch, as with the boy who cried 'Wolf, wolf!'

In conclusion, there are many ways to inculcate good values; what is obvious is that they have to be imbibed in action and that simply lecturing about various values will never succeed. It is by discussion following action that children will be able to relate them to their own behaviour; it is the dialogue and exchange of opinions that consolidate their moral stance.

Chapter VI

Promoting Positive Behaviour

'The secret of education lies in respecting the pupil.'
Ralph Waldo Emerson, Essayist

The preceding chapters have attempted to build up positive attitudes with regard to self-concept, and open feelings based on an atmosphere of security and trust. These, together with the encouragement of communication skills and the practice of discussion and dialogue, should provide a firm foundation on which positive behaviour can be based.

As implied, the positive aspect is always foremost, the aim being to develop socially conscious self-regulation where the rules and the boundaries are increasingly drawn up by the children themselves in a controlled atmosphere. This relies on the gradual acceptance of responsibility for one's own actions and an understanding of the social obligations that this implies. It has been found that when children have a real share in making the decisions about behaviour they are much more likely to be adhered to, bearing in mind that the boundaries will have to be constantly modified and extended according to age and aptitude.

This is a far cry from the old authoritarian attitude of punitive discipline, where the very word had negative connotations, and this links with the tendency on the part of well-meaning adults to point out bad behaviour rather than affirm the good. At the same time children must learn the consequences of their behaviour with a simple cause and effect logic. They need to know that if they do this then that will follow and this awareness will be an important part of self-regulation. The reality is that what one sows, one reaps; for example, if one gives happiness one gets it back in equal amounts, and vice versa.

As always, the most influential factor in determining children's behaviour is the example of the adults in their lives, particularly, of course, their parents and teachers. The atmosphere created around them needs to be tranquil and as peaceful as possible, replacing any hostility and shouting with a calm yet assertive approach and avoiding any negative exchange. Closely related to being a shining example is the practice of mutual respect: so often children protest that they are not being treated with the respect due to all human beings, and especially in the school situation they assert that 'if they respect us, we will respect them'. Furthermore, they will only really respect the adults if they 'walk their talk' and never revert to double standards – and children always know.

All of this might seem high minded, but how does it work with parents of small children and teachers with unruly classes? It is clear that young children need well-defined and consistent boundaries decided in the first instance by the parents and very gradually evolving into a certain amount of self-regulation when parents and teachers can collaborate. Early on they can learn to appreciate the consequences of their actions, being made aware of the hurt they may have caused and if possible to help repair it. This kind of retribution is a far cry from physical punishment, which is still being debated as the right of parents. This practice has been described as a radical assault on the humanity of the child as the one who metes it out is always more powerful than the one who receives it. Also, it is contradictory to tell children that hitting other children is not the way to settle disputes and then go on to smack the child who does not do what we want: a clear example of double standards. As for smacking them to protect them from danger; it may be necessary to hold them firmly until they are ready to learn to avoid accidents. Fear of punishment is no basis for motivating good behaviour, although it might seem to work in the short run. If children are treated reasonably and fully understand why the rules are made they are well on the road to self-regulation. But we, as adults, are far from perfect and reason can fly out of the window as our anger and frustration overtakes us!

Following the quiet, relaxed approach to behaviour, the procedure of 'Stop and think' has often produced good results, both in the home and school. It does not have the connotations of the more widely known, 'Time out', which can be construed as being sent to one's room as a punishment. Parents will decide how 'Stop and think' would be most effective; it can often be a well-practised habit of having a short amount of time to ponder over one's actions, even while staying in the same room.

The preceding chapters can be seen as a build-up to the promotion of positive behaviour, and parents and teachers share the same goals, although in different settings. It is interesting to know that inclusive learning centres for students with behavioural problems tend to be focused on personal and social issues, including work on anger management, relationship skills and raising self-esteem and self-confidence. It is after that stage that the secret of behavioural management, which lies in the path to self-regulation, can be explored: having one's say, gradually participating in making the rules and therefore being aware of the importance of clearly understood boundaries.

A great deal depends on the attitudes of the adults and here again the keynote is mutual respect. There was an experiment with teachers where they were given ten counters and told that they would have to sacrifice one every time they addressed a student negatively by pointing out shortcomings and unacceptable behaviour. They soon lost their counters and one wonders whether parents would have fared better. But there is no doubt that both parents and teachers are much more inclined to praise and to acknowledge children's endeavours these days, and this will also encompass the need to correct when necessary. We are more aware of the necessity to separate the deed from the doer; in other words, 'I am concerned about what you did, not what you are', and it is hard for children to tell the difference.

It is the atmosphere in the school and the home which will set the tone; if it is peaceful, relaxed and welcoming it will pay dividends, as children are quick to absorb the vibes and fit in. A teacher I know always tries to welcome her pupils as they come in and has peaceful music playing in the background.

Finally, this all adds up to a sense of security about the order of things: that there will be consistency in the rules, the sanctions and attitudes. Apparently the most troubled children are those whose adults are extremely inconsistent. In the long run their behaviour depends on how much they feel valued.

Activities

Making rules: Which school rules do you think are good? Which ones do you think are not good? If you could make up your own school rules what would they be? Should you have rules at home? Who would make them? Is there anything that you think is unfair at school? at home?

Debates on behaviour: Have formal debates on the subject of behaviour; for example, 'should children be smacked for bad behaviour?' 'Children should be excluded from school for very bad behaviour'; 'School Councils should decide on punishments for bad behaviour'; 'Children should be allowed to decide how much television they can watch'. The ideas will come from the children as they know best the areas of their concern.

Improving the school: What can children do to make the school better? Improve the playground? Improve the quality of school meals?

Cures for disruptive behaviour: in the Circle Time discuss all the ways of preventing disruptive behaviour: support from 'buddies'; family discussions; appeal that they are spoiling it for the rest. Brainstorming can produce ideas.

Respect: A Fable: In a small monastery the community was not functioning well. The Abbot says he has had a vision with a revelation that one of their group was indeed the Messiah. After that there was no dissent and everyone was compassionate to everyone else. This might be a fable for adults working together.

Active Policies for Positive Behaviour

Stifford Clays Junior School, Essex
The implementation of this policy, which I have seen in practice, is the best possible way to illustrate the living nature of positive behaviour in action.

It was produced not only in consultation with all the different members of the school community, but also was discussed with the children who were on the School Council. Children were asked about the school rules and were involved in the setting of class rules.

A major point is that relationships between children and school staff are crucial to the management of behaviour; they know that if they feel respected by staff, they will be treated fairly. They are encouraged to be independent and responsible and to develop self-discipline, and this leads them to develop self-confidence and respect for the opinion of others.

Important aims are to have a consistent approach to behaviour throughout the school and to make boundaries of acceptable behaviour clear and ensure the safety of everyone within the community. There is a list of children's responsibilities: being gentle, not hurting anybody, being polite, not being rude, moving about the school sensibly, not running, looking after property, not interfering with or damaging things, speaking quietly, not shouting and, finally, work hard, listen and concentrate. These are the golden rules. The policy on misbehaving is to give correction in a way that minimises unnecessary stress and considers the self-esteem of those being corrected. Children who have been in trouble will be given the opportunity to make a fresh start every day.

There is much more to this enlightened document, including an important role for parents to cooperate. It does give a picture of a structure that is in harmony with the best kind of education which promotes a happy and diligent atmosphere throughout the school.

Positive Behaviour in Practice
This is a detailed account of Highfield junior school, which has been dealing with positive behaviour along the lines expressed in this book. The school is situated in a non-privileged area of Plymouth and it has been practising what it preaches with respect to democracy and conflict resolution for a number of years. With the introduction of Citizenship as part of the National Curriculum, it was felt that learning about democracy and rights and responsibilities as future citizens could only be really meaningful if it was translated into living experience.

Circle Time had been long established and was becoming increasingly the forum for the children deciding and negotiating their own rules for the classroom. At the same time it was decided that each year group should have a specific goal: Year Three: self esteem and self expression; Year Four: caring for each other; Year Five: supporting others in their behaviour; Year Six: living in a democracy; and an abundance of activities and games were planned to endorse these attitudes.

Examples of types of rules agreed were: 'Follow all adult instructions'; 'Ask before leaving class'; 'No eating in class';

'No swearing'; 'Keep hands and feet to yourself'; 'Don't shout out'; etc. Of course, the making of rules did not mean that they would not be broken, and a series of sanctions were introduced for those whose behaviour overstepped the boundaries. These were in a sequence and there were plenty of warnings so that the culprits knew the increased consequences should they persist in antisocial behaviour. But they also knew what chances they had for redeeming themselves step by step by a number of days of good conduct.

The sequences of sanctions were as follows: 1) warning; 2) name on the board; 3) cross against the name and ten minutes detention; 4) another cross and twenty minutes detention; 5) talk to the Head and name in the 'Thin Ice Book', also detention every playtime and a letter to the parents explaining why they were behaving badly; this was written by the offender; 6) a final warning for further misdeeds would be the dreaded yellow card and a visit to the Head with the parents called in.

However, there was still some hope. After ten days without any wrong doing, the yellow card would be taken out of the Thin Ice Folder and a certificate of success given to the somewhat reformed offender. Comments from the pupils who had shared in establishing this formalised procedure are interesting: 'we like life to be fair and to know where we are'; 'we like to get on with our work'; 'we like to feel safe'. It might seem convoluted, but it does give the offender a whole range of chances, and the proof of its efficiency could be that virtually no children have been permanently excluded.

Moreover, a major contribution to the reform of the culprit was that house points were given for an improvement in behaviour, and classmates were encouraged to give them support. There was also a system of 'guardian angels' ready to 'fly' to the help of their protegé.

The whole system had gradually evolved from the discussions and decisions made at Circle Time in every class, and the next step was clearly a need for a whole school structure of real democracy. So a School Council was instituted with two representatives from every class, chosen sensitively with eyes closed and hands up for voting. Their role was to bring up relevant issues from their Circle Times.

A further replica of our parliamentary democracy was the election of captains from the four houses; the candidates conducting a realistic campaign in the lunch hour, based on their record, many of them having been helpful 'guardian angels', and also on their inevitable promises for future reform. All of this is contained in the Citizenship syllabus.

The secret of success in this school has been the gradual development of a system that worked, and with consultation at every level. It is still going strong. This is just one example of how to tackle behaviour problems by working as a democracy through the whole ethos of the school. Since the introduction of Citizenship, increasing numbers of primary schools are run on similar lines. Source: *Changing our School,* Lorna Farrington, Incentive Plus.

Chapter VII

Understanding Differences

*'Just as you have the instinctive desire to be happy and overcome suffering,
so do all sentient human beings; just as you have the right to fulfil this aspiration,
so do all human beings. So on what exact grounds do you discriminate?'*
from The Book of Wisdom by the Dalai Lama.

The world is full of differences which have to be understood and accepted and children need much guidance in adopting these values. We are fortunate in the United Kingdom in having many different cultures in our midst and the daily contact that our children have with them is a real opportunity to understand their ways of life, which can make for mutual empathy. On the other hand, it could also be an opportunity for racism to take hold, so it is crucial that children learn to appreciate their differences and similarities from quite an early age.

We are agreed that each person is unique and to some extent set apart from others by this uniqueness, so we need to pave the way for the acceptance of a whole gamut of variations, not only in skin colour, but in customs, ways of thinking, class, language, looks and disabilities. As racism is still prevalent, a grasp of how to deal with stereotyping and prejudice will stand children in good stead as they grow up in a multicultural society. Sexism, ageism and prejudice against disability and poverty need to be tackled in conjunction with racism, with many of the ideas and activities overlapping. So our aim in anti-bias education is to construct gradually over the years a prejudice-free understanding of people's similarities and differences and to incorporate all aspects of diversity: gender, race, economic class, ethnic background, and physical, intellectual and emotional characteristics.

From birth babies are quick to notice both similarities and differences and young children growing up focus on one thing at a time and in most cases these are the most salient features. They also tend to absorb unspoken attitudes and are quick to detect double standards in controversial areas. They think in terms of dichotomies: for example, 'like me' or 'not like me' and are prone to over-generalise. By the ages of five and six they are more inclined to imitate superheroes and become influenced by what they see on the media, and one of the reasons for starting anti-bias understanding early is that from five onwards their attitudes towards others become more consolidated. From seven onwards being included is increasingly important to them and they are developing notions of fairness and justice, so they do tend to be more tolerant and learn to stand up for themselves and others in the face of injustice. Our aim is that by this time they will be able to come to a just and comfortable relationship with diversity among people and to develop the strategies that will enable them to break the cycle of violence in their own lives and in the wider society.

In our understanding of child development we should give special consideration to the differences between boys and girls, generic as well as cultural. Contrary to many people's assumptions, boys are biologically more vulnerable than girls. Apparently, when girls are born they are already the equivalent of a four to six week old boy and this disparity continues right into adolescence. It can lead to boys being unnecessarily burdened with learning difficulty labels simply because they are slower to develop and, with the present emphasis on early learning of the so-called 'basics', which entails the constant use of language skills, boys are especially penalised.

There is also evidence of a corresponding emotional fragility. Just because they are often boisterous and full of energy it does not mean that they are not highly vulnerable in their emotional development. In fact, they need even more sensitivity and loving attention than girls to compensate for their emotional difficulties. Probably connected to these often unfulfilled needs is the fact that behavioural disorders, including problems with extreme aggression and violent behaviour, are at least twice as common in boys than in girls.

However, it is important to remember that boys have other attributes such as a heightened ability to visualise three-dimensional space, which is the key to such occupations as architecture, engineering, design and many crafts in general; also they often have higher mathematical ability. Girls tend to have greater verbal fluency and are openly empathetic in their communication skills, which gives them an advantage in much of the content of primary education and, indeed, much of what this book is advocating with regard to self-expression. Still, there is no reason why girls should not undertake work where boys have some advantage and vice versa, and this is already happening.

When these differences are understood we can give boys the extra support they need: we can encourage their special gifts in spatial development and at the same time be aware of the extra strain being put upon them in pushing them too soon in areas of literacy and language, as well as neglecting their emotional needs. This certainly requires a much more flexible approach to learning by both teachers and parents, directing it towards their particular interests and activities.

Celebrating our Multicultural Society

We all like a celebration, especially children, and the fact that there are so many diverse cultures in Britain opens up possibilities of sharing their celebrations as they will ours. The most popular ones are Divali, Id, the Buddhist and Chinese New Year and Carnival. Representatives of the various cultures can be invited to talk about their faiths and reasons for celebrating. They can be invited to Christian festivals such as Christmas and Easter; there is no better way of promoting goodwill than sharing a joyful time together. Neighbours from different cultures can be invited into the home at any time with resulting goodwill on all sides.

Sharing Food Together. We need not wait for the religious celebration to enjoy tasting each other's food and it is interesting that Indian and Chinese food are now an integral part of the British diet, with many others becoming popular, for example, Caribbean, Thai and Mexican cuisine.

World Music. There has been a proliferation of all sorts of musical instruments, not just the sitar and the steel band, from all over the world which have captivated children.

Visits to Different Places of Worship: In many parts of the country there are Hindu temples, Sikh Gundwaras and Islamic mosques to visit as well as Christian churches and cathedrals. The whole atmosphere in these places can be awesome and the art of sculptural carving and stained glass an inspiration for creativity.

Artefacts and Clothes of other Countries: Children can bring clothes for special occasions from their culture and examples of artefacts to explain their function, also illustrations of their art and sculpture. An adult can come into school and talk about their everyday life, with examples of how to wear a sari or tie a turban. For example, the organisation, 'Mexicolore' does this and children get a wonderful impression of the colourful art of Mexico, together with an idea of the intense poverty, which I saw being played out in an infant class with the pupils participating and getting really indignant at the way the landlord was cheating them out of their full pay as labourers in the fields!

Different Languages: Learn a few words such as 'Hello', 'Goodbye', 'How are you?' in the language of a classmate who will be the teacher.

Countering Stereotypes

Sexism: Changing gender: What if I became a boy or a girl? A boy and a girl each take the other's identity; the girl imagines she is a boy for a day and says what she would do and what she would be like. The boy comments on how real the portrayal was for him. Then it is his turn. Probably both would criticise the other's assumptions and this would be a good example of stereotyping and generalising.

Ageism: What would you be like when you were 65 and what would you do? Then a few sprightly 65 year olds could come and challenge their assumptions. An organisation entitled 'Growing Old Disgracefully' is very active throughout the United Kingdom and a representative might alter children's opinions of life in old age, which for senior citizens can be a new outlook featuring new relationships, creativity and a zest for life.

Prejudging Other Nationalities: What do people call the Welsh, or the Scots, Irish, or French? Would it be singers, mean or economical, fond of the whisky and naughty respectively? What do people say about the English? Would it be football hooligans, or cold emotionally? Who might have said these things? Are they right? Is what they say true of all the people of that nationality? When these ideas are taken further afield the results will probably show more stereotyping, often to the point of racism. Discussions of this kind should be conducted with great sensitivity to prevent any increase in prejudice.

Who is White and Who is Black? Children could match their own skin colour as exactly as possible with a wide range of pastels. They could trace round their two hands and colour their shade. They could then cut out their paper hands or get someone to do it for them and stick them together to make a continuum of clasped hands round the wall going from light to dark. They could conclude that no one is pure white or black.

After these kinds of activities have a discussion on what is a stereotype. A dictionary definition could be: 'when we have in mind a particular image about what a person who belongs to a certain group would be like, before we know or know of them'. This is also called a generalisation. Children's definitions would be simple: 'Just because one person is like that, it doesn't mean they all are.'

Stories

Stories are particularly helpful in initiating discussion on prejudice and stereotyping and imaginative ones about animals with the complexity of human feelings especially appeal to children.

Lily the Leopard: Lily has pink spots instead of black ones and was ostracised because of it. She becomes so desperate that she runs away and wakes up to find other leopards with a variety of spots: purple, green and orange. They make her feel quite proud of her pink spots and she goes home feeling happy about herself. (Source: Living Values)

In small groups they could make up similar stories: a pink elephant or a yellow dog. The main point to get over is how much people, who are in some way different, suffer from the unkind attacks made on them by their peers. Everyone is unique and there is great beauty in the infinite variety.

Cartoons: Older children could invent cartoons like the one with a zebra with horizontal stripes instead of vertical ones, saying with confidence to other zebras who are looking down on him, 'So what!' They could have fun drawing elephants with two trunks, rabbits with fox's tails, bears with tails like kangaroos and having the same confidence. These scenarios could be acted out in twos or threes.

Imaginary Animals: what are some imaginary creatures? – the phoenix, dragons, unicorns. Make up you own imaginary animal, either modelling it in clay or painting.

There can be prejudice against groups of people, often out of ignorance or propaganda.

Story of the Tallies and the Shorties: how in a far away country half were tall people; the Shorties called them beanstalks and looked down on them; the other half were short and the Tallies called them Shorties. One day the country became quite dark and no one could see and everyone tried to help each other and forgot to feel whether they were tall or short; they were frightened as they did not know about eclipses. When the country became light again, Shorties found they were hugging Tallies and Tallies were clinging on to Shorties. So they decided to stop discriminating and to live together happily. *Source: Living Values.*

Seeing the Other Point of View: Take a well-known fairy tale or a nursery rhyme and consider it from another point of view. For instance, what must the fairy who was not asked to Sleeping Beauty's christening have felt? She was the only one that wasn't invited. Have you ever felt left out? Did that excuse her act of revenge in casting the spell to send the Princess to sleep for one hundred years? This could lead to a discussion of whether revenge is ever right. We could talk about the story of the Three Bears. Was Goldilocks right to go into the bears' house, taste and eat up their porridge and sleep in their bed? Was it because it was just an animal's bed? In this vein the story of the maligned wolf is already well documented: about the rude little Red Riding Hood who makes personal remarks about his eyes and teeth. These can be light hearted discussions giving play to the imagination, but they could help to challenge some of the assumptions that children make, and their tendency to see characters in terms of black and white.

Children could think of other viewpoints from fairy stories or nursery rhymes: Rumplestiltskin, who is ridiculed for his disability; what about the poor spider whose home was destroyed by Miss Muffet sitting on it? Was the knave of hearts starving and should he have a right to steal the tarts?

The Two Birds: This is a story about two birds who had a dispute about what colour the leaves were in the tree they shared. The one at the top said that the leaves were green and the one at the bottom was sure that they were silver. It took a trip downwards for the bird at the top to realise that the underneath of the leaves were indeed silver and a similar change of viewpoint made the bird below finally aware of the green surface of the leaves. This scenario can be acted out. Source: *Living Values.*

The Point of View of Someone who is Different: Supposing you had a disability, how could you manage your day? In pairs try out the trust games where one is blindfold and the partner does the guiding; or plugging ears in turns to experience what it could be like to be deaf. These activities have to be treated with great sensitivity to get real empathy.

Challenging our Assumptions

Photo Analysis: The use of photographs can widen children's horizons and with discussion it can begin to question some of their assumptions. There are various photo-packs available or they can cut out their own from magazines.

Doing Things in and about the Home: This is a photo pack to promote discussion of gender stereotypes, showing men and women in unexpected roles: for example a man ironing or bathing the baby. The questions could come from the children who often ask why they are doing this and not the mother; for example, 'Is the mother ill?' showing their assumption that it is always the mother's job unless there is a crisis.

Jobs for Men; Jobs for Women: have plenty of pictures from magazines with people in them and also people working. Cut out pictures indicating work that they could be doing, for example, an engine or a nursery. Select pictures of both men and women and join them in an unexpected way; for example, a woman train driver and a man teaching in a nursery.

Discussing Photographs: Display sets of photographs depicting different ways of life in Britain and overseas and get children to ask questions about the pictures, either in pairs or in small groups. Some questions can be answered by examining the photographs carefully, others would need supplementary knowledge supplied in the photo-packs listed below. The aim is to promote understanding of different cultures, to become aware of the variations and to empathises with the people shown. 'Living with the Land' (about Ghana); 'Choices in Development' (about Tanzania and Kenya); 'Western India: City and Village Life', all from the Centre for World Development Education; also 'The World in Birmingham' (1982) Selly Oak Colleges, Birmingham B29 6LE. The slide-tape 'Unlearning Indian Stereotypes' can be used in a similar way; it depicts young Native Americans showing how the negative images commonly used about them, for example, Red Indians, savages, bloodthirsty, etc. are false.

What is this Picture About? Collect photos from magazines of scenes including people, then cut them in two making some sense of each part. In pairs show one part to the partner asking what the whole picture might be about. For example, the first picture might be of a beautiful Indian girl in a sari. The question might be 'is she a film star or a model?' The whole picture then shows that she is living in poverty in a shanty town, in a huge discarded pipeline whose circular contour made the framework of the photograph.

Group Discrimination

How would you feel if you were a member of a group that was discriminated against?

Purple and Green Bands: There was a powerful experiment in the USA dividing half the class into assumed blue eyes and the other half into brown eyes. Then they told the class that the brown eyes were not doing as well as the blue eyes and would therefore have less playtime and were picked up on anything they said or did. Halfway through they switched and said that a mistake had been made and it was the blue eyes who were so behindhand and the positions were reversed. Although it was explained that this was only pretend, the children involved were quite deeply affected and it certainly proved the point that any discrimination, even make-believe, is quite devastating. As there is a racist connection about the superiority of eye colour, in later experiments on the same lines, half the class have been given purple arm bands and the other half green ones, with no one being told why they were to wear them that day. The results were similar to the original and it gave sober truth about how harmful real discrimination is and how sensitive the issue is even if it is make-believe and only carried out for a short time.

Group Consolidation: As an antidote to the previous activity there are many games in which children form groups where they have something in common. It could be 'Huggy Bear' where they group together according to the number called out, or according to their favourite ice cream or colour. There is a sense of solidarity as they welcome someone who shares their particular preference. If there are a fair number of children participating they could group according to the month they were born in. As always, issues need to be chosen with sensitivity. Eye and skin colour are not advisable, nor who has pets, as so many families are not allowed them.

Chapter VIII

Transforming Conflicts Peacefully

'Returning violence for violence multiplies violence, adding deeper darkness to a night already devoid of stars. Darkness cannot drive out darkness, only light can do that. Hate cannot drive out hate, only love can do that.'
Martin Luther King: Chaos and Community

This section is especially important in that it presents teachers and parents with a series of concrete ways for creating an atmosphere in which children can gain the skills to solve their own conflicts. As adults we have a responsibility to inspire in our children the determination to resolve conflicts without fighting. They can learn the skills of problem solving, dialogue and negotiation with the hope that they will have their say as adult citizens in making the world a safer place.

Our children are being exposed to more and more violence and it is high time that we bequeathed to them something more positive in order to deal with this pernicious legacy. One of the main aims of this book is to guide young people into a way of life that is concerned with the transformation of their inevitable conflicts into peaceful resolution. It is largely a question of giving them confidence and the skills to help them deal with these problems so that they can enjoy happier relationships and avoid confrontations.

In the first place we must turn to the home to help them to develop the understanding and skills that they will need for living peaceably with others; then parents and teachers together can create a powerful environment for changing behaviours. Positive attitudes can be taught as effectively as negative ones if we decide to put our efforts into it, and learning to get along without violence is a skill that should be taught at an early age and reinforced and practised throughout a lifetime. Our efforts to prevent violence should begin with young children before they have learnt to accept it as a normal way of life; any attitudes and behaviour of a violent nature need to be addressed right from the start.

Alongside this direct approach we need to reinforce the strategies contained in the previous chapters which play a significant role in achieving any successful transformation of conflictual situations. These are the tools that our children need to deal with their inevitable confrontations: the ability to state clearly your point of view and to be able to listen attentively to the other one, and particularly to be able to express your feelings with confidence.

In some ways very young children have a head start with these attributes; they can be uninhibited about stating their case and their feelings. It is often later that their self concept gets knocked and their feelings bottled up. On the other hand, to be able to listen and to understand the other's point of view is something that has to be learnt as they develop. So with an understanding of young children's development we can appreciate their forth-rightness in stating their case and having no inhibitions about 'telling tales', and we can rejoice at their apparently innate sense of injustice. At the same time we can be aware of the fact that young children find difficulty in realising that others can feel as much hurt as they do, so they need experiences that reveal to them what other people are feeling and to tolerate differences.

Another relevant aspect of young children's thinking is the tendency to deal entirely with opposites: one's own point of view is the right one and the other's is the bad one, and much of what they see on television endorses this outlook. The good guys have to eliminate the bad guys and they are justified in carrying out this mission with as much violence as possible. This mentality is prone to be carried on into adult life and in the political arena. So children need to understand that there are many points of view, not all good and not all bad, and that in order to formulate their own opinions and attitudes they must engage in mutual dialogue with others.

What can we do as parents and teachers to help them deal with the daily differences of opinion that they will encounter, which could so easily lead to confrontation? As ever, the most potent way is patently obvious: by setting a good example. Yet this is not easy to carry out from day to day. All children, and especially young ones, model their behaviour on that of the adults around them, so if we can remain calm and just in our dealings with others, especially in any conflictual situations, they will respond accordingly, at least in the long run, and this is the most valuable support that we can give them.

But before we can hope that they become the reflections of our attempts at modelling perfect behaviour, there are many well-tried strategies to help them on their way. There is an accepted formula to deal with conflict, which can be adopted in the home and in the classroom with the help of an impartial mediator, provided both parties agree. This incorporates the possibility of both protagonists giving their point of view about what happened and for them to express their feelings on the matter. Then, using their imagination, they brainstorm all possible solutions to their problem, including ones that are not really feasible. Finally they are challenged to agree on the best solution they both would like to happen, without being forced to compromise; in other words to arrive at a win-win solution. What is important at every stage is that the other contestant is expected to repeat or summarise what their opponent has said in order to prove that they have really listened to and understood it.

This formula might seem too directive, but it has been well tried with successful outcomes. If it appears too cumbersome the mediator might limit the repetition to one statement each. However, if taught at a young age, it can become accepted almost automatically. Children feel safe with some structure that they can rely on and, after rehearsing it in the form of simulated role-play, they can begin to use it with the help of a mediator in real life situations.

The Use of Role Play

Probably the best method of learning to consider the other's point of view is through role-play, already a popular feature of their imaginative play from the earliest years.

Role-play with Puppets

Role-play gives children the opportunity to rehearse their behaviour in real life, especially when they find themselves in conflictual situations. The use of puppets can be both helpful and enjoyable for young children; they could make quite simple 'Me' ones with just a photo or self-portrait stuck onto a lollypop stick or a mitten, and later they could enlarge their repertoire to include their family, or the characters in the conflict role-played, or from a story.

It is best to keep the role-play as simple as possible, with children first getting to know their 'Me' puppets, talking to them and getting replies, singing together and having a chat with their neighbour's puppet. Some children may prefer to make simple animal puppets and create scenarios around them. There is no need for a theatre in the early stages, but if there is enough room, a designated corner where children can go and play puppets would be welcome.

The conflict resolution scenario procedure would be guided by

the teachers or the parents and it is important to get it right from the beginning, as it is a rehearsal for the real thing. It is best if the adults enact the role-play to begin with, as it will be more structured than in spontaneous play and some children will probably be too shy to start acting.

After a few examples of conflict being suggested by the adults, the children could brainstorm scenarios, as they are the ones that really know what happens in their relationships. For example, quarrelling over the use of a toy, perhaps a tricycle; spoiling or breaking toys, books, paintings, homework, clothes; borrowing these items without permission, and possibly harming them; dispute over which television programme to watch; in a shared room, one wanting quiet to do homework and the other to play a CD; accidental harm to someone, e.g. knocking them over; older siblings being bossy, younger ones being a 'pain'; all these and many more! Later, the bullying problems could be played out: name calling, pushing, hitting, harming clothes, taking money, etc.

Dramatic Role-play on the Resolution of Conflict

It is a good idea first to act out the incident as it really was, then replay and stop before it gets to the original outcome; it is helpful if the action can be recorded on video, but not essential. Brainstorm the possible solutions and act out the most positive ones. Which one will be a win-win solution? At first the alternatives offered by the participants will tend to consider only one point of view, but it will become evident that one must be found that is equally fair to both sides. They have to learn to distinguish between their needs and their wants; for example, 'I need to be asked before my things are borrowed'. The choice of a solution will depend on needs expressed by both sides rather than individual wants, and this is where the practice of 'I messages' rather than 'You messages' can be helpful.

Assertiveness Training

This is a basic approach that will stand children in good stead in their personal relationships and especially in conflictual situations. The rules for being assertive are quite simple and they can be taught both in discussion and in simulated experiences. They are: to know what you want to say and be able to say it clearly and firmly. Body language is of paramount importance; for example, the stance you make with your whole body and looking the person straight in the eye. The technique is knowing how to stand up for yourself, both physically and internally. You need to know and practise a variety of responses and to know how to use them appropriately. For example, someone who is vulnerable and in danger of being a victim could learn to say, 'Stop!', or 'I don't want you to do that!', with firm resolve; and many conflict situations demand that there is effective yet positive confrontation which can be learnt in this way. There are many other ways of asserting oneself in a difficult situation, such as whistling, deliberately walking away with head held high; it is only with practice that the right attitude is hit upon.

In conflict resolution being asked what you would like to happen is a way of asserting yourself without violating the integrity of either party. It creates options whereas an accusation produces a defensive response which further escalates the problem. On the other hand, giving in and not asserting oneself can increase resentment. Basically, assertiveness training is to go with the flow with 'I' statements telling how you feel about something: 'When you yell at me I feel ...' and what would be your preferred outcome: 'I'd like it if I could have ...'

Role Play on Assertiveness: In pairs list the things that could be criticised in someone else; for example, clothes, hairstyle, accent, spectacles, parents, etc. Learn to say, 'I don't like it when you make fun of my ...'; or more briefly, 'Get lost!', or 'So what?' A group dealing with appearance differences has coined the phrase, 'What's the point you're making?', or 'I don't get the point', and this would be for a slightly older age group. Participants would take turns in playing both roles.

Real Life Conflict Resolution

With the build-up of plenty of experience in playing out imaginary conflicts, it is easier to tackle those that occur on a daily basis. It must be recognised that this will be a sensitive area for the protagonists, so when in doubt role-play could still take its place as being once removed. Moreover, in the heat of the moment children are not likely to remember the strategies for a win-win solution; they may be asked if they would like to have a mediator straight away or they may need to calm down in a quiet room for a time.

The Role of the Mediator

Children will already be familiar with the procedure of conflict resolution in their role-play scenarios. In most cases the mediators will be the adults to begin with, but there is a growing tendency to train children in peer mediation, some even as young as eight years old. The process is always voluntary, but this does not mean that any conflict will go unheeded; it always needs to be followed up and resolved. In the school situation, usually in the playground, when they are given the choice between peer mediation and being referred to the teacher, it is not surprising that they choose their peers. Whether teachers or students, the formula is basically the same as described earlier: What happened; how do you feel? What could be a solution? Agree on the best solution that would satisfy all concerned and pledge to carry it out.

The mediators have strict rules they need to enforce; for example, no name calling and no put downs; no violence and no interrupting; try your best to solve the problem; pledge to carry out what you have promised to do with regard to the final solution. They also have their own rules: they must be impartial and never take sides; they should not tell people what to do; they should not talk too much and they must preserve confidentiality. In their training mediators are helped to frame sentences that will make bridges of communication: for example, 'I think you might feel'; 'Maybe we could try'.

They need to clarify the respective roles, theirs and the contestants; they steer the process and the disputants supply the content. If they give suggestions these are merely options and never directions; they can reframe after listening to ask, 'Can you think of what you could do so that you would both feel safe and happy?' Of course, if the contestants are young or even if they aren't, egocentric solutions will follow, but the mediator needs to stay with the children until they have managed to agree to a mutually satisfactory solution. In this way the children are helped to express their ideas and to feel responsible. Drawing on their creativity they could be asked 'What could you do if this happened again?' This scenario entails a certain amount of time spent, which may be possible in the home or with trained nursery and classroom assistants in school if the student mediators have to refer it.

The existence of a peace corner or peace table is a great asset in this process. It can be used for a cooling off period, for talking things over with a sympathetic person or giving an opportunity for a couple in confrontation to work things out for themselves, record the nature of the dispute and then write in the book provided what they have agreed. Whether in the home or school it should be situated in as private a place as possible with something of beauty to adorn it: a special cloth, comfortable chairs, flowers to create an atmosphere of tranquillity.

The results of mediation have been extremely good, whether carried out by adults or peer-group students. It is heartening to know that when young people have been trained in peer mediation, they have been very successful, as indeed is often the case when we trust children with responsibility. In fact a number of junior schools are already giving sessions in mediation techniques, then electing mediators with reference to their suitability and enthusiasm for the privilege.

Brainstorming

As brainstorming plays such an important role in the peaceful resolution of conflicts, it is worth reminding ourselves of the process. The rules are quite strict; everyone has the opportunity to contribute as long as they take it in turns; no one is allowed to comment on anyone's ideas; suggestions can range from the practical to the far-fetched and imaginative but never hurtful. To practise brainstorming children can concentrate on impartial ideas such as, 'How many uses does a piece of string have?' (Edward de Bono, 1971), and they can make up their own similar questions.

The Role of the Adult in Conflict Resolution

Parents and teachers play a crucial role in guiding the children in their care to deal with their conflicts successfully. Perhaps the most relevant example they can give is to remain calm and tranquil with a clear but quiet voice and certainly no shouting. Their advice is constantly to use words to resolve confrontations and never to resort to physical retaliation even of the mildest character.

Ideally the adults should be aware of incipient hostility; as with most confrontations there is a great deal going on before it becomes apparent and the build-up is hardly noticed except by the participants, but when it passes the threshold and becomes open conflict, it is only then we see fit to intervene. As ever, prevention is better than cure and an early discussion of the issue will make it easier to resolve. We can always remind children at this stage that they really want to be friends again, although they might not agree in the heat of the moment. If one has been really hurt there could be some kind of reparation to acknowledge the bruised feelings and if the gesture came from the adult in charge, the other party would feel less blamed. It could be a gesture such as being allowed to take home the class pet for the weekend.

It is helpful for adults to have some understanding of child development and to be aware of the fact that young children do not always recognise that others get hurt just as they do, both mentally and physically. One of the most salient pieces of recent research shows that if the grownups always point out this reality to young children, they are much more likely to have compassion for others. As usual research seems to be stating the obvious, but it's good to have our natural empathy for others confirmed.

By the time children are five or six their feelings are easily hurt and in a competitive world it is difficult for them to lose. They are very eloquent but need help in finding words to express their feelings in resolving their conflicts. By the time they are seven or eight they need to feel that they are in control of the situation in order to save face and here the formalised structure of conflict resolution can be used with great advantage, as both parties can negotiate so that both can feel like winners.

This approach can be contrasted with a more disciplinarian attitude; for example when we instinctively impose our decisions on the conflict, which is sometimes essential, say to separate two who are engaged in a physical struggle. But there are other occasions when we could choose between putting both parties in 'time out' and negotiating. A way in to the formal structure might be to say, 'You are both really upset. What's the problem?' and turn conflict-creating statements into non-provocative questions. We can write down agreements, acknowledge the participation of the contestants and congratulate them on their success in resolving the problem. We can confer with any 'buddies' or guardian angels, which are now quite regularly used amongst peer groups to support any children who may be vulnerable. Older peer mediators have sometimes taught self-esteem games and even established one-to-one counselling, after appropriate training. They certainly have helped to reduce bullying and have improved the general feeling of safety in the school.

Activities: What should we do?

List a number of conflicts: e.g. You are being blamed for spoiling someone's work, trainers or for tripping up a player in a football game. The accused is innocent and the incident was an accident. In threes use the conflict resolution formula, probably giving the accused the benefit of the doubt if he or she is genuinely sorry. They could discuss reparation such as an apology, putting right the damage done where possible or a small gift.

Tableaux: First, in pairs, one models a negative emotion and the other changes it into a positive one by adjusting the body posture and the expression. Three people make a series of mediation tableaux, then mime it, but do not talk. Discuss afterwards what it was about and how it was resolved. In two groups of three or four take turns in making a tableau of a gang bullying a child. The other group alters the statues until they have stopped the violence.

Paint a picture of anger. Draw two cartoons showing a scene where someone was made to feel very angry and then someone else making it alright.

Freedom from Bullying

Probably the most deadly form of conflict is bullying, which is prevalent in schools in spite of valiant efforts by many teachers and parents to deal with it constructively together. Nevertheless, we can certainly make life a whole lot better for the many children who suffer from it: those who are bullied, the onlookers and also the bullies themselves. The attitude of many teachers and parents until recently has often been that bullying in school has been a traditional factor throughout the centuries and in every country and that little can be done about it. Parents have been inclined to encourage their offspring to fight back and teachers have assumed that their pupils need to sort out their problems themselves.

Now there is clearly a change taking place where incidents of bullying are the responsibility of everyone concerned: teachers and helpers, assistants, supervisors, parents, children and also the wider community. There is an obligation for every school to adopt a 'Whole School Policy', which entails a firm commitment on the part of everyone working in the school to apply a specific code of behaviour aimed at eradicating all kinds of bullying, whether physical, mental or a subtle combination of both. The policy also implies close cooperation with the parents, who are often the first to be aware of the possibility of their child being bullied.

The preparation we have made in leading up to the peaceful resolution of conflicts will stand us in good stead in an onslaught on any form of bullying: the need for self-assurance on the part of potential victims and indeed the onlookers and even for the would-be bully, who, with all of their swagger, is possibly feeling inadequate inside.

The school described in the chapter on positive behaviour has a very well defined policy on bullying. They first started with a Bully Box for students to post into, saying what happened; it could be anonymous, but always with the colour code of the class concerned. The contributions were then discussed in Circle Time and students were asked to bear in mind that 'bullies were people who chose the wrong behaviour'. They would decide whether the accusation seemed fair and if it should be pursued by the teachers.

Later they found that the box was no longer needed, as cases were referred straight away to the House Captains, who by then had been properly trained in the mediation process and in some instances had their own 'clinics'! If the problem was not resolved it was referred to the Schools Council and if necessary the parents and teachers would be involved, with the cooperation of all concerned.

Action on Bullying

What is Bullying? Brainstorm which could include: displays of aggressive behaviour towards others; verbal abuse and threats, any menacing actions causing fear; upset or worry in the hearts and minds of other children.

Discussion on Bullying: Brainstorm any of the following questions: 'How might a bully feel?'; 'What would you say to a bully?'; 'How would someone who was being bullied feel?'; 'What would you say to that person and what could you do for him or her?' 'What would you do if you saw someone else being bullied?' In the discussion the fact that it is right to tell would probably emerge quite strongly. The children could draw pictures to illustrate these occurrences with themselves taking on the various roles of bully, bullied and onlooker. In threes act out the roles having made up an imaginary situation.

Listing: With the brainstorming procedure make lists: for example, 'What are some of the things that bullies do?'; 'Where are the most likely places that bullying takes place?' The teacher could contribute the less recognised bullying tactics; for example, hidden insults by a group towards a victim; it could be an imperceptible indication of a smell when near the victim which no one notices except the one targeted. Discussion would follow, as in the next activity.

'It's right to tell': this is the message that generally emerges from the discussion and if it does not, adults can state their viewpoint on the basis of how can they help if they are left in the dark? The accumulated value of these discussions will have a group consciousness of the need to eliminate bullying in all of its forms.

Talk to Bullies: This would be a follow-up after the above discussions and be in private with the teacher and later with the parents, concentrating on the fact that their behaviour will not be tolerated. The bully should be treated with firmness, but with understanding so that he is not humiliated; at the same time, he needs power over others and that can never be allowed.

Hassle Line: In pairs stand opposite each other in line. First have one side saying 'Yes' to their partner and the partner responding 'No!', with half a minute before they change roles. They could progress to a simple bullying incident: One calls the other innocuous names and these are agreed before hand such as 'you are a fiddle-de-dee'! or 'a dilly dally'!, avoiding sensitive issues such as permanent features or racist accusations. Differences in tone and volume of voice could be discussed, emphasizing how important it is to keep one's calm.

Cat and Mouse: For this fantasy there needs to be a peaceful atmosphere with the children sitting or lying comfortably. The adult describes how you come across an empty house and go into a dark empty room. You suddenly believe you are changing, getting much smaller and growing a tail and whiskers with a long nose, and you realise that you are turning into a mouse! Then a large cat enters the room! What are your feelings? Just as the cat is ready to pounce, you are both changing roles and now you are the cat. How do you feel now? Can the children make up and act similar stories: a deer and a lion; a frog and a crocodile? These can all be acted out with one person telling the story and couples being the cat and mouse.

Chapter IX

Educating Young Citizens

'Your children are not your children
They are the sons and daughters of Life's longing for itself.
…
You may give them your love but not your thoughts:
For they have their own thoughts.
You may house their bodies but not their souls, for their souls dwell in the
house of tomorrow,
Which you cannot visit, not even in your dreams.
You may strive to be like them, but seek not to make them like you.'
From The Prophet by Kahlil Gibran

There could never be a more appropriate time to set young children on the path of citizenship. What does it mean to be a good citizen? First, to be a well rounded integrated person; secondly to be able to relate to others in a caring way, and thirdly to participate fully in the rules and regulations based on the value system of the society.

We have now run the gamut of the ingredients which help to prepare children to become socially conscious members of society. Perhaps the most important factor is always that they should be happy and that entails providing as secure an environment as possible, both in the home and at school. This will be the basis for their good self-regard, which is a prerequisite for having good relations with the people around them and gradually the wider community.

Their practice of discussion in the Circle debates and group work later on will give them the skills to produce the power of independent judgement and the ability to express themselves clearly and with confidence. Having a say in the rules and boundaries is essential for self-regulation, which must be the aim of every adult, both to be prepared to keep to the rules of society and to be active in trying to alter them if they are unreasonable.

Furthermore, practice in electing one's own representatives, albeit on a micro scale, lays the foundation for participation in a truly democratic state. They are not too young to be aware of the difference between autocratic and democratic rule, they have probably experienced it already; and the fact that their opinions are worthy of being considered will strengthen their support in the future.

They are also not too young to play an active part in making their voices felt in community matters on issues relevant to them. It is well known that children are concerned about conserving the environment, for example, sometimes putting the adults to shame.

Good citizenship implies foresight and planning and also being aware of the consequences of one's actions, and we all need to face the future in order to be in control of it, as far as this is tenable. Often fear can dominate thoughts of the future and it will help young people if they can discuss these feelings and how to overcome them.

Teachers and Parents Working Together

The introduction of Citizenship in the National Curriculum has opened up greater possibilities for collaboration between teachers and parents. Fortunately, there is a good deal of cooperation between the home and school these days and this is particularly important in the gradual build-up to educating future citizens. Together they are in charge of the most formative years of the children in their care and this can only be really effective if they are closely in touch with each other right from the earliest years. This partnership is paramount with regard to attitudes to behaviour. For example, if the school has a punitive approach to misbehaviour and the home a positive, self-regulating one, or vice versa, then there is a two-tier standard which is very difficult for children to cope with. The same need to collaborate is even more relevant in relation to their standpoint on conflict-resolution. If the parents are saying 'Hit him back' to a victim of bullying and the school is dedicated to teaching techniques of mediation, it puts great stress on the child concerned.

With close consultation as equal partners responsible for the well-being of the children in their care, these differences can often be worked out; and this is the overriding theme of having opportunities to discuss differences. They are united in wanting the best for their children and it is by contact and close consultation that they will be able to get some consensus. Of course, their methods will vary greatly and by its very nature the school situation would be more structured, whereas in the home there would be the day-to-day influence of living closely together. It would be good if teachers were allotted more time to confer with parents, particularly in the light of the addition of Citizenship to the curriculum.

Putting Citizenship into Practice

What is most exciting about citizenship education are the opportunities for children to get thoroughly involved; they could be asked to take the assembly, run a school newspaper, or contribute towards school policies, such as an anti-bullying campaign. They might be asked to take part in discussion groups on, for example, how much television they should watch.

Children's learning is concerned with action and they will understand the real meaning of democracy if they experience it. The curriculum recommends some form of school's council and in many schools this is practised. It can be instituted with, say, two representatives from each class, one boy and one girl, chosen with eyes closed for voting, and their role would be to bring up relevant issues from their Circle Time. A further replica of our parliamentary democracy would be the election of house captains, with realistic campaigns for votes and the usual promises for future reform if they were elected. On the website www.explore.parliament.uk there is a complete set of resources to enable you to run an election in school, with three fictitious parties, manifestos and ballot papers.

Children can take more responsibility in running the school; besides cooperating with or actually making the rules, they can also have individual jobs such as taking care of pets or plots, with badges awarded making them feel valued and an integral part of the school community. They have even been known to take part in the interviewing of new teachers with considerable success. Apparently the question they were most likely to ask was what the teachers could contribute in the way of extra-curricular activities.

Many schools have been able to remake the asphalt playgrounds into sustainable and enjoyable areas with the participation of the pupils and often their parents. One such has described the 'bleak, tarmac wastescape' being turned into a wonderland with the help of 'Learning through Landscapes' and community artists. It incorporated the following features: a 'castle', stage, peace garden, water feature, gallery for the children's work, plus mosaics made by the pupils. In other playgrounds the pupils have constructed a sundial on the ground. In other, similar ventures students have worked with an ecology group to help with a programme of sustainability. This has provided valuable experience of the real world of decision making and teamwork. For younger children there is a growing number of Forest Schools in close proximity to woodland, where they learn about protecting the environment.

Parents who might be involved in a campaign could talk to their children about it and even involve them if the children so desired. Such protests as demanding a zebra crossing near the school, or protecting trees in danger of being cut down to make way for a car park, or a motorway through the town, are well within the children's interests, and their participation could give them confidence that their voices will be heard. There can be debates on similar protests with public opinion against the authorities, with the formality of the debating system simplified according to the age group of the children.

Visits to Institutions: The Houses of Parliament is an obvious one for citizenship education and children should be aware of the right to see their MP, especially if there is an issue within their scope. I once took my whole class to meet our local MP and their questions were all far-reaching and relevant. In Nottingham the old county jail has become an education centre and children visiting can get a real insight into the old procedures: a Victorian courtroom, an Edwardian police station with a wealth of arte-facts and, most impressive of all, the fact that this was the build-ing where the reform bill rioters and Luddites were tried and executed on the steps outside.

The Rights of the Child

Introduce the idea of the rights of the child. Ask, what are rights? Something that in all fairness you are, or feel you are, entitled to? Brainstorm what should be included in a list of children's rights and write each suggestion on a card. In groups of three sort out copies of the cards to choose the ten best from the point of view of the group. They can then team up with another group and try to get agreement as to which ideas would go through to make up the top ten. This is a good exercise in give and take.

Then present them with the United Nations Declaration on the Rights of the Child:

U N Declaration on the Rights of the Child (1959)

The right to affection, love and understanding.

The right to adequate nutrition and medical care.

The right to free education.

The right to full opportunity for play and recreation.

The right to a name and nationality.

The right to special care, if handicapped.

The right to be among the first to receive relief in times of disaster.

The right to be a useful member of society and to develop individual abilities.

The right to be brought up in a spirit of peace and universal brotherhood.

The right to enjoy these rights, regardless of race, colour, sex, religion, national or social origin.

The ten points agreed by the groups will probably have quite a few differences from the UN declaration. They will probably be more materialistic, such as the right to more pocket money or to have a bedroom of one's own. How would they alter their version in the light of the United Nations Declaration? Would they add more? I personally would add the right to have a sustainable environment.

One new right that has been added to the Convention on the Rights of the Child is particularly relevant to the curriculum on Citizenship: 'Children should have the right to express their views on all matters of concern to them and to have those views taken seriously in accordance with their age and maturity'.

This right has always been denied to children and it is only in recent years that their opinions are being listened to and acted upon where reasonable. It is heartening to know that the stance made in this book is backed by the new United Nations' declaration.

Your Special Right: A group of children can be asked what they would like especially to have as a right. They can draw an illustration and dictate what they would like to write if necessary. When a group of primary school children were given this exercise it was quite revealing; they mostly voted for love, 'Let's always have love', with pictures of a mother cuddling her child. 'Time for a hug'; 'Cuddles are free!' There was also a strong plea for safety: 'Protect me from fire; … from animals', these accompanied by drawings of fierce creatures ready to pounce on a helpless child and a fireman carrying a child down the ladder from a high rise block of flats.

In some cases they are helped in their writing and drawing by the adults, but the ideas were all theirs. There were also pleas for play: 'Remember to have fun with us' and 'Let me be messy sometimes'. There were heartfelt cries to be listened to: 'Listen to us!', with a picture of an enormous ear, and, perhaps the wisest of the lot, 'Remember that you can learn from us too'. This being aptly illustrated by a drawing of an adult wedged in a tiny desk and a child in front teaching her! Finally a demand for fair play: 'Everybody should have a turn in feeding the hamster'!

This is yet another example of the depth of children's thought that can emerge when they are treated seriously and with respect.

Working with the Community: Special Projects

The Pyramid Trust: There are growing numbers of local community projects and it is well worthwhile for teachers and parents to find out about them and take advantage of their help. One such example is the National Pyramid Trust, a charity whose aim is to arm vulnerable children with the tools they will need to get through the difficult business of moving from primary to secondary school, concentrating on building their confidence and self-esteem.

The organisers say that fun is the name of the game and that having fun means being relaxed and making friends and eventually trusting each other enough to talk about their fears. The project is based on four ingredients: love and security, new experiences, praise and recognition and responsibility. The results have been quite amazing; children who were really shy have changed into leaders both at games and in discussions. National Pyramid Trust: www.nptrust.org.uk

Environmental Awards: There are a number of environmental projects which give awards to schools for their practice in respecting the environment. One such takes place annually in London with five themes: litter; waste and recycling; energy; transport and biodiversity. The schools are judged on, among other things, how much their pupils are involved with their own initiatives and how imaginative their projects are.

The children become litter detectives, design ways to save energy, have 'walk to school' weeks and make part of the school grounds more appealing to plants and wildlife. The teachers have said that this is an inspiring way to lay the foundations of responsible citizenship and it will challenge even very young children to make environmentally friendly choices at school and at home; certainly the children have responded with enthusiasm to the challenge.

In Your Neighbourhood: This is a project that pupils in a primary school in Hampshire undertook to improve their school grounds; the result was that vandalism and graffiti disappeared. It has now been extended to the community, looking at their area, discovering problems and reporting them to the council.

With an award they have bought equipment to record their findings, which include interviews with local residents to get their opinions on what should be changed. The children have gained in self-confidence and are learning to work together, and when something gets done as a result of their efforts they have a great sense of achievement.

School meals: There are initiatives to improve the quality of schools meals to wean children off the ubiquitous diet of chips and pizza. In Cornwall there is a project involving over a hundred schools to have entirely local products for their meals, involving the children in choosing what (healthy!) food they want and getting their opinions about it afterwards. This idea can reduce the traffic carrying goods long distance and also create less pollution. The pupils are made aware of the importance of promoting local products at a time when they are often bypassed in favour of goods from overseas.

Car Chaos: A primary school in Suffolk has been doing a traffic survey to see whether children as good citizens can come up with ideas to help alleviate the traffic problems. They have been awarded some money, which they have spent on equipment for filming and photographing to back up their concrete suggestions to the parish council.

In these projects it will be the older children who will carry out much of the research, but efforts are made to involve the younger ones as much as is feasible, and they will be prepared to continue the work as they grow older. The pride of being listened to and treated with respect permeates the whole school and sets the tone for confidence that citizens, even young ones, can effect change when it is necessary.

A Sacred Space: This is a local community based project at present in Berkshire called The Lighthouse. The inspiration came from a bombed out shell of a cathedral, where the rescued stained glass windows had been constructed into an eight-sided room for people to come and sit in peace in a haven of light and colour.

This is their stated aim: The whole purpose of The Lighthouse is to create a sacred space where young people can experience Peace. What does peacemaking mean? What are **my** conflicts? How can they be resolved? We believe that this can best be done in an octagonal yurt which they have helped to build and then decorate with images of Peace they themselves have depicted. Ideally, these images will be created on eight transparent panels so that the space becomes filled with Light. There is a direct comparison with the architecture of other sacred spaces like a Church, Temple, Gurdwara, Mosque, etc., where Light illuminates the visions of humankind portrayed in windows and icons. Here, eight distinct groups of young people (from a community, a youth club, a school, perhaps in time an offenders' institution or a refugee/asylum centre) are invited to explore a space and the concept of spaciousness, mediating it with their own creativity and so coming to 'own' it through their own work. The respect each group expects for their own work develops into respect for the work of others and hence for people in other groups as they are encountered. In this way, mutual respect is enhanced and then reinforced by the peacemaking processes* shared within what will become, if sensitively hosted, an increasingly sacred space. [* These might include silence, prayer, guided meditation, singing, nonviolent conflict transformation techniques such as circle time, mapping, the arts of listening, etc.]

Different community groups, including schools, have got together, each to create a panel out of stained glass (well, actually Perspex) as a mindful reflection of their desire for peace. The panels from the groups are assembled in a circular tent, a yurt, radiating colour and light. This is The Lighthouse, which will tour around schools and community groups, its members facilitating workshops and giving presentations on living peace, using the tools of conflict resolution, and compassionate communication as well as creativity and silence.

The yurt will then be available at the school for students to use as a quiet space during the rest of the week and the aim will be for the school to be inspired to construct their own peace haven, or something similar, according to the means at their disposal, always with the possibility of community involvement. This project supplements the ideas in Chapter 3 on Creativity and the great need that children have for a space in which to be tranquil and at peace.

Looking to the Future

Time Lines: Draw a life line labelling it with the special events in your life: e.g. going to nursery/infant/junior school; moving house; a holiday. In pairs, share it with your partner as a listening exercise.

My Future: Draw two lines starting from the present, marking one with what you think will happen and the other with a vision of what you would like to happen. Again share in pairs if it is not considered too private. Each one chooses one item in each line to talk about; in the first line it might be fear of another war and in the other a vision of a peaceful world, or more likely having lots of money!

War and Peace: What do you think of when people speak of war? What do you think when people talk about peace? Could you draw or paint two pictures, one of war and the other of peace. In pairs, talk about your pictures. Then ask the question, 'what could people do to stop having a war?'

The School that I'd Like: Brainstorm all the features you would like in your school then sort out the ones that could become a reality. The Guardian competition on this subject had 15,000 replies and most of them were answers to practically every dilemma that the education system is currently grappling with. For instance, at their ideal educational establishment every child would be eager to attend and so there would be no problem of truancy or exclusion. Of course, there were some outrageous flights of fancy such as the distribution of free lipsticks with each school meal, which could be a part of any brainstorm. But, as the winner of the 1967 competition said, 'It proves yet again that young people are not a problem that needs to be corralled and curfewed, but an incredible rich resource of wisdom and creative thinking that we should learn to listen to'. So this is yet another plea to listen to children and respect what we hear. Ref. *The School that I'd Like?* Burke, C. & Grosvenor, I, Routledge Falmer.

Schooling in Finland

At this stage I should like to describe some of the features of the Finnish education system, which seem to be in harmony with much of what I am advocating in this book.

As in many European countries, formal schooling in Finland does not start until seven, being preceded by kindergarten for all children. They continue in the same school until they are sixteen, when only 3 per cent of students decide to end their schooling. 70 per cent continue with their academic studies, 27 per cent go on to vocational schools and between 60 and 70 per cent go on to the university or polytechnic.

The guiding principle of Finnish education, according to the senior adviser at the ministry, is student-centred democracy. There is no selection involved at any stage and students are free to choose, within reason, what they want to study. The board of education lays down a National Core Curriculum and schools are able to timetable and teach it in whatever way they think best, and creativity is encouraged at every stage. Although there are internal exams, there are no SATS, GCSEs or ASs, which certainly makes for less stress. The only national examinations are at the end of their school careers, usually at age 18 or 19.

What is really interesting in all this is that Finland leads the world in the international league tables (Organisation for Economic Cooperation and Development (OEDC) and came top of the world's literacy rankings in the July (2003) OEDC/ Unesco Programme for International Student Assessment report. Ref: Crace John, Heaven and Helsinki. *Guardian*, 16.9.03.

Changes in the Primary School

There are positive signs that the British education system, with its rigid implementation of the National Curriculum, the proliferation of external examinations and the corresponding hierarchy of league tables, might be moved to make changes along the lines that this book puts forward.

The highlight in this approach is the syllabus on the relatively new subject of Citizenship, which many good schools have always been practising: building better relationships between staff and pupils; form and school councils with a say in how the school is run; the supporting of close links between the school and the community. The foundation stones of citizenship are experiential learning, moral responsibility, community involvement and political awareness, and these can be laid in the primary school. There are also increasing lobbies to give creativity its proper place as the backbone of all learning, with inspiration and imagination an essential if not the most important ingredient if education is given rightful priority in terms of support.

Having welcomed the possibility of some change, it is necessary to acknowledge that a much more comprehensive restructuring of the whole current educational system is necessary. I sincerely hope that by the time this book is published SATS at ages 7, 11 and 14 will have been abolished; an aim voiced by the teachers' unions and a ground swell of educationists and parents.

These relatively small improvements are only a beginning.

In order to give our children the education they deserve, there must be much more commitment to a radical change in investment in education. Children need to be given full consideration as unique individuals and this means smaller classes and an approach to learning that is not tied to a rigid syllabus geared to a series of examinations.

If I had one wish, which would make a vast improvement throughout the schooling system, it would be for much smaller classes. This would help facilitate all the aims of this book.

Childhood, whether at home or at school, should be a happy time with real interest in learning and joy in playing, and we have the means to make this ideal a reality if education is given its rightful place in terms of priority and support.

Epilogue

A Visit to a Positive School:
Forty Hill CE Primary School, Enfield.

Schools can have souls just like human beings and the one we visited had a particularly vibrant spirit. To me it was a living testimony of what this book is about. From the moment one entered the doors there was an atmosphere of peace and tranquillity as a background to a hum of purposeful activity.

Ours was not a formal visit; just wandering around in the afternoon taking photographs for this book of anything that was going on, and what was happening was a sure illustration of the ideas the book contains.

What we experienced were sessions of Circle Time where the pupils were able to express their feelings to each other in a natural environment shaded by trees with logs to sit on. There were two outdoor classrooms areas; one specially used for Circle Time and general discussion, and the other with tables with benches and a large blackboard on a wall for children who wanted to have a quiet breaktime. Only the rain would prevent them from being used; unless it was really cold they could have their coats on. The whole area had been laid out by a joint effort of teachers, parents and students, with a large pond separating the two areas. When they had just finished the pond with all of its plants, a couple of wild ducks came immediately to claim it and built a nest. The children were thrilled; a teacher described to me the hilarious day when they covered the whole area with bark shavings, all joining in, pouring it out of the sacks and raking it even.

By this time it was the turn of the classes that we had been watching to go to dinner: in the hall they formed a most orderly, quiet queue with one or two of the older pupils looking after us. The choice was really appetising; roast lamb and gravy, creamed potatoes and savoury cabbage, which was all my choice; an alternative was pasta, the seconds were fruit salad, ice cream, jelly or pudding, or a combination of these, all served by ladies who obviously took pride in their cuisine and the children's obvious enjoyment of it. We sat with them and I must say 1 have never seen such a big slice of lamb being thrust into such a small mouth, but it went down all right! There were small plastic cups filled with pure juice to help wash it down. 1 have gone into some detail to show how school lunches can have a good influence on children's eating habits, which have now gone so drastically astray with the resultant obesity.

The concomitant factor of exercise was also addressed; and in the field next to the outdoor classrooms we found the older children organising games for the young ones; they were doing this so effectively that I felt that they might become teachers themselves one day. They were clearly modelling themselves on the staff, who were relaxed and at the same time well organised and efficient. The most striking aspect of the teacher-pupil relationship was the mutual respect that they had for each other.

Then there was a games period and the large, colourful para-chute was brought out on to the field. Here the 'buddy' system, practised throughout the school was especially apparent. The older pupils all adopted a younger buddy and looked after them when needed. With the parachute games, they mostly alternate small and tall as they each held on to the edge. These games are a great exercise in cooperation and whether it was getting the parachute as high as possible in the air or acting together to control the large, plastic ball, they all managed to contribute.

We left them to the fresh air and saw a drama lesson where the teacher was encouraging them to improvise a fairy story on the platform. Behind them was the scenery made cooperatively by the children of a fairy-tale castle with turrets and battlements, set against an azure sky. Finally we saw the end of a painting lesson where the children were painting imaginative themes with great intensity. What really struck me was how they managed to share one paint-box between three without any kind of tension: they seemed to dip as they needed and the colour remained quite clear.

Then we had a talk to the Head Teacher, who had joined us from time to time, having a word with the children and staff as we wandered round. Back in his study, he told us about the more formal lessons in the morning: he felt that it was possible to take the literacy and numeracy periods in their stride, especially as there had been an easing of the prescriptive approach. They were getting good results, especially at the older stage when the benefits of postponing formal 'basics' teaching until later were apparent. The Ofsted inspection had been highly satisfactory and they were right up in the league tables. It was living proof that this approach produces good results in learning and most importantly learning with enjoyment.

The Head talked of the application of new research on the brain, which revealed the multi-faceted nature of everyone's ability to learn. The staff were all conscious of children's different modes of learning, whether visual, auditory or kinaesthetic and the importance of treating each child as an individual.

Of course there were bound to be problems, but it seemed that they were dealt with immediately and any suspicion of potential bullying was stamped out before it began. For children who found real difficulty in adjusting there was a full-time Inclusion Teacher who had time to understand and guide them and it was significant that there were no cases of exclusion from school.

There are a number of clubs that are organised in rotation in order to provide variety of choice. At present there are netball and rounders clubs and football for the young children, card and board games, country dancing and nature detective clubs, which are all pursued enthusiastically.

The attractive newsletter gives an idea of the close co-operation between the school and the parents, who are certainly playing a very active role in the school life, especially in funding the many projects including the outdoor areas, shrubs and plants.

This is only a bird's eye view of the school, but it has been enough to convince me that this is the **'School that I'd like'**.

Bibliography

Adams, John, 1979, *Games Children Play around the World,* Toys Ltd.

Aesop, 1995, *Aesop's Fables (The Boy Who Cried "Wolf"* and *The Tortoise and the Hare),* translated by S. A. Handford, Penguin Popular Classics.

Alderman, Carole, 1995, *Sathya Sai Education in Human Values, Book 1 Ages 6-9 years,* Sathya Sai Education in Human Values of the UK, Pinner, Middlesex, UK.

Alderman, Carole, 1995, *Sathya Sai Education in Human Values, Book 2 Ages 9-12 years,* Sathya Sai Education in Human Values of the UK, Pinner, Middlesex, UK.

Antidote, 2003, *The Emotional Literacy Handbook,* David Fulton. www.fultonpublishers.co.uk and www.antidote.org.uk

Axeline, Virginia, 1969, *Dibs in Search of Self,* Ballantine Books.

Belloc, Hilaire, 1995, *Matilda,* from *Cautionary Verses,* Red Fox.

Berrien Berends, P, 1983 *Whole Child/Whole Parent,* Harper& Row.

Bettelheim, B, 1986, *The Uses of Enchantment,* Knopf, New York.

Bettelheim, B, 1987, *A Good Enough Parent,* Pan.

Blishen, E, 1969 (ed), *The School That I'd Like,* Penguin.

Brahma Kumaris, 1995, *Living Values: A Guidebook,* Brahma Kumaris, London, UK.

Brahma Kumaris, 1992, *Visions of a Better World,* Brahma Kumaris, London, UK, pp. 8-9.

Britton, J, 1972, *Education Towards Freedom,* Pelican Books.

Brooks, Jane B, 1994, *Parenting in the 90s,* Mayfield Publishing Company, Mountain View, USA.

Bruner, Jerome S., 1966, *Towards a Theory of Instruction,* Norton.
    1964, *On Knowing. Essays for the left hand,* Harvard University Press.
    1983, *Under Five in Britain,* Blackwell.
Buckman, P, 1973 (ed), *Education Without Schools,* Souvenir Press,
    London.
Buckton, Chris, 1980, *The Experience of Parenthood,* Longman.
Burns, Sally & Lamont, Georgeanne, 1995, *Values and Visions,* Hodder
    and Stoughton, London.
Burke C. & Grosvenor I, 2003, *The School that I'd Like,* Routledge Falmer.
Beaver, Diana, 1997, *Easy Being: Making Life as Simple and as Much Fun
    as Possible,* Useful Book Company, UK.
Buzan, Tony, 1974, *Use Your Head,* BBC Books, London.
Carey, D and Large, J, 1982, *Festivals, Family and Food,* Hawthorn Press,
    Stroud.
Children of the World, 1994, *Dear World: How Children Around the
    World Feel About the Environment,* Bodley Head Children's Books.
Children of the World, 1994, *Rescue Mission: Planet Earth,* Peace Child
    International; Kingfisher Books, London.
Citizen Foundation, 2002, *Young Citizen's Passport,* Hodder and
    Stoughton, UK.
Coplen, D, 1982, *Parenting,* Floris Books, Edinburgh.
Crace, John, 2003, 'Heaven and Helsinki', *The Guardian,* 16 September.
Crowe, B, 1986, *Play is a Feeling,* Unwin.
Crowe, B, 1986, *Young Child and You,* Unwin.
Day, Jennifer, 1997, *Children Believe Everything You Say,* Element Books,
    Shaftesbury, Dorset, UK.
De Bono, Edward, 1983, *The Mechanism of Mind,* Penguin,
    Harmondsworth.
Deacowe, J, 1982, *Sport Manual of Non-competitive Games,* Family
    Pastimes.
Department for Education and Skills, www.dfes.gov.uk/citizenship/
Dinkmeyer, Don & McKay. Gary D, 1976, *The Parent's Handbook,*
    American Guidance Service. Circle Pines, MN, USA.
Doing Things in and about the House. 1983, Photographs and Activities
    about Work, Play and Equality, Serawood House.
Elkind, David, 1981, *The hurried child. growing up too fast too soon.*
    Addison-Wesley Pub. Co.

Faber Adele & Mazlish, Elaine, 1980, *How To Talk So Kids Will Listen & So Kids Will Talk,* Avon Books, New York.

Farrington, Lorna, 2002, *Changing our School,* Incentive Plus, PO Box 5220, Great Horwood, Milton Keynes, MK17 OYN.

Fisher, Pat, 1986, *Remember the Light,* Fenton Valley Press, Storrs, Connecticut.

Gardner, Howard, 1999, *Intelligence Reframed. Multiple Intelligences for the 21st Century,* Basic Books, New York.

Goleman, Daniel, 1996, *Emotional intelligence. why it can matter more than IQ. Emotions,* Bloomsbury, London.

Goodman, P, 1971, *Compulsory Miseducation,* Penguin, London.

Grimm, J, 1975, *The Complete Grimm's Fairy Tales,* Routledge, London.

Haim, Ginott, 1969, *Between Parent and Child,* Avon Books, New York.

Haller, I, 1987, *How Children Play,* Floris Books, Edinburgh.

Hawkes, Neil, 1996, *School Policy,* West Kidlington Primary and Nursery Schools, Oxford.

Holt, J, 1970, *How Children Learn,* Penguin, London.

– *How Children Fail,* 1971, Penguin, London.

– *Instead of Education,* 1976, Penguin, London.

– *Learning all the Time,* 1989, Lighthouse Books.

Human Values Foundation, 1994, *Education in Human Values: Lesson Plans 1-3 Truth, Love, Peace,* Human Values Foundation, Ilminster, Devon, UK.

Human Values Foundation, 1994, *Education in Human Values: Lesson Plans 4-5 Right Conduct, Non-violence,* Human Values Foundation, Ilminster, Devon, UK.

Human Values Foundation, 1994, *Education in Human Values: Manual,* Human Values Foundation, Ilminster, Devon, UK.

Jones Lynn, 2003, *Young Citizen's Passport: Your Guide to the Law in England and Wales,* Hodder Arnold, London.

Judson, S, 1983, *A Manual on Non-violence and Children,* New Society Publishers.

Knight, M et al, 1982, Teaching *Children to Love Themselves,* Spectrun.

Kreidler, W, 1984, *Creative Conflict Resolution,* Scott Foreman.
   1990, *Teaching Concepts of Peace and Conflict,* Educators for Social Responsibility, Cambridge, MA, USA.

Large, M, 1990, *Whose's Bringing Them Up?* Hawthorn Press, Stroud.

Lennon, John, 1971, *Imagine,* Parlophone Record Company, UK.

Living Values: an Education Programme, 2000, *Educator Training Guide,* UK.

Living Values: an Education Programme, 1999, *Facilitator Guide for Parent Values Groups,* UK.

Living Values: an Education Programme, 1999, *Values Activities for Children Ages 3 - 7,* UK.

Living Values: an Education Programme, 1999, *Values Activities for Children Ages 8-14,* UK.

Living Values: an Education Programme, 2000, *Values Activities for Refugees and Children-Affected-by-War,* UK.

Living Values: an Education Programme, 2000, *Values Activities for Young Adults,* UK.

Living Values: an Education Initiative, 1996, *Living Values Cards,* CASA Productions.

Mandela, Nelson, 1995, *Long Walk to Freedom,* Abacus (Little, Brown).

Masheder, Mildred, 1989, *Let's Play Together,* Green Print, London.

– 1990, *Windows to Nature,* World Wide Fund for Nature.

– 1994, *Let's Enjoy Nature,* Green Print, London.

– 1997 3rd edition, *Let's Co-operate,* Green Print, London.

– 1989, Video *Let's Co-operate-* Illustrative cooperative and Parachute Games, 75 Belsize Lane, London NW3 5AU

– 1998, *Freedom from Bullying,* Green Print, London.

Mainland, Pauling 2003, *A Yoga Parade of Animals,* Element Children Books

Merrill, Charles, 1985, *Freedom to Learn,* Carl Rogers.

Miller, A, 1987, *For Your Own Good,* Virago, London.

Montessori, M, 1969, *The Absorbent Mind,* Dell New York

Mosley, Jenny, 1993, *Turn Your School Around a Circle Time approach to the development of selfesteem,* L.D.A, Chris Lloyd Sales & Marketing Service, UK.

Mosley, Jenny and Sonnet Helen, 2002, *Games for Self Steem,* LDA.

National Pyramid Trust: www.nptrust.org.uk

Peachey, J Lorne, 1981, *How to Teach Peace to Children,* Herald Press.

Pfister, Marcus, 1992, *The Rainbow Fish,* North-South Books, New York, USA.

Piaget, Jean, 1962, *Play, Dream and Initiation in Childhood,* Norton, New York.

1977, *The Moral Judgement of the Child,* Penguin, Harmondsworth.

Postman, N and Weingartner, C, 1971, *Teaching as a Subversive Activity,* Penguin, Harmondsworth.

Provenzo, E F, 1991, *Video Kids: Making Sense of Nintendo,* Harvard University Press, Cambridge, Mass.

Prutzrman, P, et al, 1978, *The Friendly Classroom for a Small Planet,* Avery Publishing Group.

Ramsay, Barbara, 1995, *Finding the Magic,* Eternity Ink, Sydney, Australia.

Rogers, C, 1983, *Freedom to Learn for the 80's,* Charles E Merrill.

Russell, B, 1926, *On Education,* Allen & Unwin.

Silverstein, Shel, 1964, *The Giving Tree,* Harper Collins, USA.

Skynner, R and Cleese, J, 1983, *Families and How to Survive Them,* Methuen.

Sokolov, I & Hutton D, 1988, *The Parents' Book,* Thorsons.

Steiner, R, 1971, *Human Values in Education,* Rudolf Steiner Press, Bristol.

Teachers' Guide, *All about Me,* Schools, 1977, Council Health Education Project, Nelson.

The Times, article by Rowan William, Tuesday 23 July 2003 pp. 2-4.

UNESCO: *United Nations Year for Tolerance,* 1995, Office of Public Information, UNESCO, Paris, France. Available at the UN Bookstore.

Walker, P and F, 1988, *Natural Parenting,* Bloomsbury, 1987, and Inter-link, New York.

Weare, Katherine, 2000, *Promoting mental, emotional, and social health. A whole school approach,* Routledge, London.

Whitaker, Patrick, 1993, *Practical Communication Skills in Schools,* Longman, Harlow.

Williams, Rowan, 2000, *Lost Icons. Reflections Cultural Bereavement,* T. & T. Clark, Edinburgh.

Winnicott, D, 1964, *The Child, the Family and the Outside World,* Penguin, Harmondsworth.

Warnock, Mary, 1998, *An intelligent person's guide to ethics,* Duckworth, London.

United Nations: 1992 *The Universal Declaration of human Rights – An Adaptation for Children,* UN Publications, New York, USA.

Organisations

Antidote, 45 Beech Street, Barbican, London EC2Y 8AD.

Association for Citizenship Teaching, www.teachingcitizenship.org.uk/

Learning through Landscapes, 3rd Floor, Southside Offices, The Law Courts, Winchester, S023 9DL, schoolgrounds-uk@ltl.org.uk and website: www.ltl.org.uk

Living Values, Brahma Kumaris, 3 Fullamoor Cottages, Clifton Hampden OX14 3DD. www.bkpublications.com

Sapere, Dialogue Works, Northmead House, Puriton, Somerset TA7 8DD.

The British Wheel of Yoga, 25 Jermyn Street, Sleaford, Lincs NG34 7RU

The Circle Works, 6 Temple Yard, Temple Street, Bethnal Green, London E2 6QD.

Mediation UK, Alexander House, Telephone Avenue, Bristol BS1 4BS

World Aware, formely the Centre for World Development Education (CWDE), Croydon High Street, Croydon, UK

Also by Mildred Masheder:

Let's Play Together
An exciting collection of over 300 games and sports which put cooperation before competition – and make everyone a winner!
You'll find traditional party games, circle games, musical, board and guessing games, games for the lively and energetic, for the drama-minded or the artistic, nature games, and parachute games.
Playing games will never be the same again!
1854250132   £8.99

Let's Co-operate
This book contains many ideas for parents and teachers to share with their children. With sections on: a positive self-concept, creativity, communication, co-operation, getting on with others and peaceful conflict resolution. Illustrated with photographs and drawings.
1854250906   £6.99

Let's Co-operate Video
A lively and colourful video which illustrates many of the games in *Let's Play Together*. It includes popular games such as 'Dragon's Tail', 'Lapsit' and 'Blind Partners', and also explores the delights of parachute games, including 'Mongolian Tent', 'Sharks', and 'Cat and Mouse'.
The video is informative as well as pleasurable to watch and can encourage parents, teachers and club leaders to try out parachute games.
Parachutes as shown in the video are also available for sale on inquiry to the address overleaf.
£9.99

Let's Enjoy Nature
A book to help parents, teachers and their children get in touch with nature and care for the planet.
With over 500 ideas for activities including: making things from nature; conducting experiments; growing plants; nature games; seasonal celebrations; exploring the countryside; conservation in the home and beyond.
With 150 illustrations.
1854250922   £8.99

Freedom from Bullying

This is a practical book designed to help teachers and parents work with children to prevent bullying at school from nursery to secondary stage, and deal with it when it occurs.

Conclusive evidence shows that co-operation between parents, teachers and children can free a majority of pupils from a scourge that has plagued countless generations.

1854250922   £8.99

All available from Mildred Masheder at the address on the next page, or from good bookshops (except the video).

Let's Co-operate Pack

This pack is suitable for teachers and parents of children aged three to fourteen years.

The overall approach is experiential, with ideas, activities and games on co-operation in the classroom, the home and in the wider context of caring for the natural world.

- *Freedom from Bullying*
- *Let's Play Together*
- *Let's Enjoy Nature*
- *Let's Co-operate*
- *Let's Co-operate Video*, which illustrates many of the games in *Let's Play Together* and explores parachute games.

The pack is available for £50 including postage. Please send a cheque to:

Mildred Masheder, 75 Belsize Lane, London NW3 5AU
Tel. 020 7435 2182
Individual titles are also available from Mildred Masheder (please add £2 per title postage & packing) or from good bookshops

Visit the Merlin Press/Green Print web site:
www.merlinpress.co.uk